GETTING STARTED
WITH SPANISH

GETTING STARTED WITH SPANISH

Beginning Spanish for Homeschoolers and
Self-Taught Students of Any Age

WILLIAM E. LINNEY
ANTONIO L. ORTA

ARMFIELD ACADEMIC PRESS

Published by Armfield Academic Press

Editorial consultant: Scottie Sue Brittain
Editorial consultant: Alejandro Miranda
Editorial consultant: Ana Avilés
Editorial assistant: Geraldine Linney

ISBN-13: 978-0-9795051-3-3

ISBN-10: 0-9795051-3-5

Library of Congress Control Number: 2009901519

CONTENTS

Preface vii

How to Use This Book ix

Lessons 1-177 1

General Advice 217

Answer Key 219

Pronunciation Guide 269

Glossary 271

Subject Index 277

PREFACE

My previous book, *Getting Started with Latin*, was a labor of love. I wrote it to help homeschooled and self-taught students learn beginning Latin at home, without a teacher. Since the publication of *Getting Started with Latin*, the response has been nothing but positive (well actually, there was that one nasty e-mail...but never mind about that). Anyway, people seem to like the one-thing-at-a-time format of the book, which never leaves them lost and wondering what just happened like other books do.

This is significant because homeschooled and self-taught students are a special group of people who need specialized materials—products that allow folks to learn at home without access to a teacher. So when I saw the positive response to *Getting Started with Latin*, I wondered if I could also apply that same step-by-step approach to a modern language such as Spanish. While I was writing *Getting Started with Latin*, I joked with my old friend Antonio Orta that we ought to write a Spanish book together after the Latin book was finished. After joking about it a couple of times, we started to realize, "Hey, that actually sounds like a pretty good idea!" So now, after a lot of dreaming, scheming, and even some hard work, our beginning Spanish book is a reality.

The basic format used in this book is designed to accomplish several educational goals. We have designed this book to:

- Be self-explanatory, self-paced, self-contained and inexpensive
- Allow the student to make progress with or without a Spanish teacher
- Provide plenty of practice exercises after each new concept so the student can master each idea before moving on to the next one
- Provide a full array of audio recordings for aural practice and supplementary instruction
- Avoid making beginning Spanish any more difficult than it actually is

Getting Started with Spanish was created to meet the unique needs and preferences of homeschooled and self-taught students. It is self-contained, with no extra materials to purchase (such as pronunciation tapes, answer keys or teachers' editions). It's also in a large format to make it easier to use, as well as nonconsumable so it can be used with multiple children. The answer key is in the back of the book, and there are free pronunciation recordings and authors' commentary recordings available for download at www.GettingStartedWithSpanish.com. In this book, new words and concepts are introduced in a gradual yet systematic fashion. Each lesson provides many exercises for practicing the new material while reviewing material from previous lessons.

Getting Started with Spanish makes beginning Spanish as accessible as possible to students of any age or educational background. Because this book moves so gradually, students probably will not say *This is too hard for me. I quit!* Instead, these bite-size lessons should leave the student encouraged and ready to continue. But when you do finish this book, don't let your Spanish studies end there. Learning and using a foreign language is quite a thrill—so keep going and above all, have fun with it!

William E. Linney

HOW TO USE THIS BOOK

This book is structured around one main teaching method: Teach one concept at a time and let the student master that concept before introducing the next one. With that in mind, read the tips listed below to help you use this book to the greatest advantage.

THE NEW WORD

Start each lesson by observing the new word for that particular lesson. All Spanish words in this book are in **bold print** so they will be easy to recognize. The meaning of the new word is in *italics*. In some lessons you will learn a new concept and in others you will simply review material from previous lessons.

PRONUNCIATION

The best way to learn correct pronunciation is by listening and copying what you hear. Visit www.GettingStartedWithSpanish.com to download the free pronunciation recordings in MP3 format. In these recordings, each new word and exercise is read aloud by native speaker and co-author Antonio Orta. You may listen to these recordings on your computer or put them on a CD and listen to them on any CD player. Either way, these free audio recordings will help you achieve proper Spanish pronunciation.

Occasionally, there will be a written pronunciation tip at the beginning of a particular lesson. These tips are included in the book to prevent some of the most common pronunciation errors. To assist you further in achieving proper pronunciation, there is a pronunciation chart on page 269 for the sake of reference.

GRAMMATICAL INFORMATION

If needed, a lesson may contain an explanation of how to use the new word introduced in that lesson. Charts and examples will be used to give the reader a clear presentation of the Spanish grammar knowledge needed for that particular lesson.

In addition, the website has commentary recordings, specially prepared by the authors, that cover each lesson in detail. So if you have any trouble understanding the material presented in a lesson, you will have plenty of help on hand.

THE EXERCISES

Armed with the knowledge of the new word and how to use it, the student should then begin to translate the exercises. In a homeschool environment, it is probably best to have students write their answers in a notebook. Older students and adults may prefer to do the exercises mentally. Next, turn to the answer key in the back of the book to see if your translations are correct. By comparing the Spanish and the English, you will be able to learn from your mistakes. Translating the exercises over and over will enhance learning and speed progress.

PRACTICING CONVERSATIONAL SKILLS

Now comes the really important part. Once you understand the exercises, it's time to practice using and understanding what you have learned. The ideal situation would be to have a family member or friend with whom you can practice Spanish on a daily basis. Repetition is the key here. Try repeating the exercises over and over to each other or making up your own similar sentences.

If you can't practice with a friend or family member, you can still accomplish a lot by practicing with the pronunciation recordings. You can practice your pronunciation skills by trying to pronounce the exercises just like the speaker. Or, you can practice your listening skills by repeatedly listening to and interpreting the recordings.

SPANISH COMPOSITION

For an additional challenge, you can try to translate the answers back into Spanish using the knowledge you have gained from that lesson. This is called Spanish composition. Figuring out how to write something in Spanish can be a great learning tool because it requires the student to think about the material in a different way. Try it and see! Again, it is probably best to write these exercises in a notebook.

DON'T PUT THE CART BEFORE THE HORSE

Do not skip ahead to a future lesson. Because each lesson builds directly on the preceding lessons, the student should do the lessons in the order given. If you start to feel lost or confused, back up a few lessons and review. Or, take a break and come back to the material at a later time. Remember that review and repetition are essential when learning any language. One of the best things you can do to improve your understanding of Spanish is to review the lessons repeatedly.

STAY FLEXIBLE

Everyone has a different learning style, so use this book in ways that fit your needs or the needs of your students. You can learn Spanish as a family, on your own, or in a homeschool environment. Be creative! You could even have one night of the week when the entire family is allowed to speak only Spanish. Who knows? You may think of a way to use this book that no one else has thought of (putting it under the short leg of the kitchen table does not count).

TESTS AND QUIZZES

To give a student a test or quiz, simply back up to a previous lesson. Have the student translate those exercises without looking at the answers. Then, the teacher or parent can grade the exercises using the answers in the back of the book. Another possibility would be to test the student's listening skills by having him or her translate the exercises directly from the audio recording for that lesson.

SCHEDULING

Some homeschool parents like a lot of structure in their teaching schedules, while others prefer a less structured learning environment. Depending on your personal preferences, you may either plan to cover a certain number of lessons in a certain period of time, or allow your students to determine their own pace. It's up to you.

HOW MUCH TIME PER DAY?

A few minutes a day with this book is better than longer, less frequent sessions. Thirty minutes a day is ideal for language study. Of course, this may vary with each student's age, ability and interest level.

SELF-TAUGHT ADULTS

Adults who use this book will enjoy the freedom of learning Spanish whenever and wherever they please. High school and college students can use it to get a head start before taking a Spanish class, to satisfy curiosity, or to try something new. Busy adults can use it to study at lunchtime, break time, or while commuting to work (as long as someone else is driving the vehicle). The short lessons in this book will fit any schedule.

SURF THE NET!

The website that accompanies this book (www.GettingStartedWithSpanish.com) has free resources to aid you in your study of Spanish. Be sure to check it out!

LESSON ONE

ARTICLES

Articles are words such as *the*, *a*, and *an*. Let's take a look at some examples:

> The man
> The woman
> A chair
> An apple

A noun is a person, place or thing. In each of the examples above, we used an article to introduce each noun.

In the next few lessons, we will learn how to use articles in Spanish.

LESSON TWO

GENDER

In Spanish, each noun is either masculine or feminine. This quality that nouns have is called *gender*.

This concept is easy to understand with people and animals—after all, we know that animals and people are either male or female. But in Spanish, even words for non-living things have gender. For instance, pencils, cars, and houses all have gender in the Spanish language.

So whenever you learn a Spanish noun, you need to remember the gender of that word—that is, whether it is masculine or feminine.

LESSON THREE

NEW WORD **el**

MEANING *the*

In English, the word *the* is always the same. No matter what word it introduces, the word *the* is always just *the*. In Spanish, however, there is more than one word for *the*.

In Spanish, there is a masculine form of the word *the*, and a feminine form of the word *the*. So if you have a masculine noun, and you want to put the article *the* in front of it, you must use the masculine form of the word *the*.

El, our new word for this lesson, is the masculine form of the word *the*. In the next lesson, we will use **el** to introduce a masculine Spanish noun.

A WORD ABOUT PRONUNCIATION

Spanish pronunciation is not the same as English pronunciation. The best way to learn correct pronunciation is by listening and copying what you hear. Be sure to visit www.GettingStartedWithSpanish.com to download the free pronunciation recordings in MP3 format. In these free audio recordings, each new word and exercise is read aloud by native speaker and co-author Antonio Orta. You may listen to these recordings on your computer or MP3 player, or if you wish you may put them on a CD and listen to them on any CD player.

Also, there is a Spanish pronunciation guide on page 269 for the sake of reference.

LESSON FOUR

NEW WORD   **niño**

MEANING   *boy*

PRONUNCIATION TIP: The little mark over the letter *n* is called a *tilde*. In Spanish, whenever the letter *n* has a tilde over it, it will sound similar to the *ny* in the word *canyon*. So **niño** sounds like *NEEN-yo*.

Niño is our first Spanish noun. It is masculine, so if you want to put the article *the* in front of it, you must use **el**, the masculine form of the article *the*.

EXERCISES:

  1. **Niño**
  2. **El niño**

When you see the exercises in each lesson, try to translate them on your own. The answers are in the back of the book to keep you from peeking.

And don't forget to listen to the pronunciation recordings, too.

The answers to this lesson are on page 219.

LESSON FIVE

NEW WORD   **la**

MEANING   *the*

You already know that **el** is the masculine form of the article *the*. Now it is time to learn the feminine form.

La, our new word for this lesson, is the feminine form of the article *the*. In the next lesson, we will use **la** to introduce a feminine Spanish noun.

In the meantime, please take a moment to examine this simple chart.

MASCULINE	**el**
FEMININE	**la**

LESSON SIX

NEW WORD **niña**

MEANING *girl*

PRONUNCIATION TIP: The little mark over the letter *n* is called a *tilde*. In Spanish, whenever the letter *n* has a tilde over it, it will sound similar to the *ny* in the word *canyon*. So **niña** sounds like *NEEN-ya*.

Niña is our first feminine Spanish noun. Since it is feminine, if you want to put the article *the* in front of it, you must use **la**, the feminine form of the word *the*.

EXERCISES:

1. **Niña**
2. **La niña**
3. **Niño**
4. **El niño**

Answers on page 219.

LESSON SEVEN

NEW WORD **y**

MEANING *and*

PRONUNCIATION TIP: This word, which has only one letter, sounds like the *e* in *me.*

EXERCISES:

1. **Niño y niña**
2. **Niña y niño**
3. **El niño y la niña**
4. **La niña y el niño**
5. **El niño**
6. **La niña**

Answers on page 219.

LESSON EIGHT

NEW WORD   **un**

MEANING   *a* or *an*

PRONUNCIATION TIP: This new word sounds similar to the word *moon*, except without the *m*.

We already know how to say *the* in Spanish, and now it's time to learn how to say *a* and *an*.

What is the difference between *a* and *an*? Please examine the following examples:

A̲ book
A̲n̲ apple

A and *an* are actually the same word but with one important difference: *a* comes before words that begin with a consonant and *an* comes before words that begin with a vowel. Why the variation in spelling? This is done in order to make pronunciation easier. For example, it is easier to say *a book* than *an book*. Likewise, it is easier to say *an apple* than *a apple*. So try to think of *a* and *an* as two variations of the same word.

Un, our new word for this lesson, is the masculine form of the word that means *a* or *an*. We use it to say *a* or *an* before masculine nouns.

EXERCISES:

1. **Niño**
2. **Un niño**
3. **El niño**
4. **Niño y niña**
5. **La niña**
6. **El niño y la niña**
7. **La niña y el niño**

Answers on page 219.

LESSON NINE

NEW WORD   **hermano**

MEANING   *brother*

PRONUNCIATION TIP: In Spanish the letter *h* is always silent. So **hermano** sounds like *er-MAH-no.*

Hermano is masculine, so it needs to have a masculine article like **el** or **un**.

EXERCISES:

1. **Hermano**
2. **Un hermano**
3. **El hermano**
4. **Niña**
5. **La niña**
6. **Niño**
7. **El niño**
8. **Un niño**
9. **El niño y la niña**
10. **La niña y el niño**

Answers on page 220.

LESSON TEN

NEW WORD   **una**

MEANING   *a* or *an*

PRONUNCIATION TIP: **Una** sounds similar to the word *tuna*, except without the *t*.

Una is the feminine version of **un**. We use it to say *a* or *an* before feminine nouns. Examine the following chart:

MASCULINE	**un**
FEMININE	**una**

Now we know how to say *a* or *an* before masculine and feminine nouns. Let's get some practice with all the articles you know by translating the following exercises.

EXERCISES:

1. **Una niña**
2. **Un niño y una niña**
3. **Una niña y un niño**
4. **Un hermano**
5. **El hermano**
6. **La niña**
7. **El niño y la niña**
8. **Un niño**
9. **El niño**
10. **La niña y el niño**

Answers on page 220.

LESSON ELEVEN

NEW WORD **hermana**

MEANING *sister*

PRONUNCIATION TIP: In Spanish the letter *h* is always silent. So **hermana** sounds like *er-MAH-na.*

Hermana is a feminine noun, so it needs to have a feminine article such as **la** or **una.**

EXERCISES:

1. **Una hermana**
2. **La hermana**
3. **Un hermano y una hermana**
4. **La hermana y el hermano**
5. **Un niño**
6. **Una niña**
7. **Un niño y una niña**
8. **El hermano y la hermana**
9. **La niña**
10. **La niña y el niño**

Answers on page 220.

LESSON TWELVE

NEW WORD **mi**

MEANING *my*

PRONUNCIATION TIP: **Mi** sounds similar to the English word *me*.

Mi is always the same—in other words, it doesn't change for each gender.

EXERCISES:

1. **Mi hermana**
2. **Mi hermano**
3. **Mi hermano y mi hermana**
4. **El hermano**
5. **Un hermano y una hermana**
6. **La hermana**
7. **La niña**
8. **El niño y la niña**
9. **Una hermana**
10. **Una niña**

Answers on page 221.

LESSON 13

NEW WORD **tu**

MEANING *your*

PRONUNCIATION TIP: **Tu** sounds similar to the English word *to*.

Tu is always the same—in other words, it doesn't change for each gender.

EXERCISES:

1. **Tu hermana**
2. **Tu hermano**
3. **Mi hermano**
4. **Tu hermano y tu hermana**
5. **El niño**
6. **Una niña y un niño**
7. **Mi hermana**
8. **La hermana y el hermano**
9. **La niña**
10. **Mi hermana y tu hermana**

Answers on page 221.

LESSON 14

NOUN ENDINGS

Please take a moment to compare the nouns **niño** and **niña**:

niño
niña

Did you notice anything special about these two nouns? **Niño** and **niña** are the same except for the last letter. **Niño** is the masculine form (meaning *boy*) and **niña** is the feminine form (meaning *girl*). The masculine form ends in **–o** and the feminine form ends in **–a**.

Let's also take a moment to compare **hermano** and **hermana**:

hermano
hermana

Again, with **hermano** and **hermana**, we see that they are the same except for the last letter. The masculine form of the word ends in **–o** and the feminine form ends in **–a**.

Many Spanish nouns (but not all) follow this pattern. So be on the lookout for them!

LESSON 15

NEW WORDS   **amigo / amiga**

MEANING   *friend* (male) / *friend* (female)

In the last lesson we talked about pairs of nouns in which the masculine form ends in **–o** and the feminine form ends in **–a**. So, instead of giving you **amigo** in one lesson and then **amiga** in another lesson, we are going to give you both of them at the same time.

Use the word **amigo** for a *friend* of the male gender, and **amiga** for a *friend* of the female gender.

EXERCISES:

1. **El amigo**
2. **La amiga**
3. **Un amigo**
4. **Una amiga**
5. **Tu amiga**
6. **Mi amigo**
7. **Mi amiga y tu hermana**
8. **Mi hermano**
9. **La niña y el niño**
10. **Mi hermano y tu hermana**

Answers on page 221.

LESSON 16

NEW WORDS   **muchacho / muchacha**

MEANING   *young man / young woman*

Any of several words could be used to translate the word **muchacho** into English: *boy, young man, kid,* etc. But in this book, just to keep things simple, we will translate **muchacho** as *young man.*

And **muchacha**, the feminine form of **muchacho**, can mean *girl* or *young woman.* But in this book, just to keep things simple, we will translate **muchacha** as *young woman.*

EXERCISES:

1. **Una muchacha**
2. **Un muchacho y una muchacha**
3. **El muchacho**
4. **La muchacha y el muchacho**
5. **Mi amigo**
6. **La amiga**
7. **Tu amiga y tu hermano**
8. **El niño y la niña**
9. **Tu hermana**
10. **Un niño**

Answers on page 222.

16

LESSON 17

SINGULAR AND PLURAL

Singular means there is one of something.

Plural means there is more than one of something.

Just for practice, try to figure out if the underlined word in each sentence is singular or plural.

EXERCISES

1. I have three <u>cats</u>.
2. Hand me that <u>book</u>, please.
3. I saw a <u>deer</u> in the woods.
4. I want to catch a <u>fish</u>.
5. There are many <u>cars</u> on the road today.
6. I need a new <u>pair</u> of pants.
7. The <u>deer</u> are eating all of my plants!
8. We don't have any more <u>cookies</u>.
9. The <u>fish</u> are in the fishbowl.
10. We painted the wrong <u>house</u>.

Answers on page 222.

L E S S O N 18

PLURAL NOUNS

In the last lesson, we learned the difference between singular and plural. In Spanish, so far, we have studied only singular nouns. But in this lesson, we are going to study plural nouns.

This is how to make a noun plural: If the noun ends in a vowel, simply add the letter *s*, as in the following example.

Hermana *(sister)* becomes **hermanas** *(sisters)*

If the noun ends with a consonant, add *es* to the end of the word. We have not seen any nouns like that yet—but when we do, we will practice making those words plural, too.

For practice, see if you can make each of these words plural.

EXERCISES:

1. **Muchacho**
2. **Niña**
3. **Amiga**
4. **Niño**
5. **Muchacha**
6. **Hermana**
7. **Amigo**
8. **Hermano**

Answers on page 222.

LESSON 19

GROUPS OF MIXED GENDER

A *friend* of the male gender is an **amigo**. A *friend* of the female gender is an **amiga**. A group of male *friends* is a group of **amigos**. And a group of female *friends* is a group of **amigas**. But what happens if you have a group of friends that includes both males and females? What word would you use for them?

So far we have seen several Spanish nouns that have a masculine form and a feminine form (such as **niño/niña**, **amigo/amiga**, and **hermano/hermana**). With nouns like these, *whenever you have a group that includes both males and females, you use the masculine form to refer to the group.* So if you had a group of *friends* made up of both males and females, you would call them **amigos**. Even if it is a group made up mostly of females with only one male present, you still must use the masculine form.

Likewise, a *brother* is an **hermano**, and a *sister* is an **hermana**. A group of *brothers* would be **hermanos**, and a group of *sisters* would be **hermanas**. But what if you want to refer to a group of people that included *brothers* and *sisters*? Again, you would use the masculine form, which in this case would be **hermanos**. So in that context, the word **hermanos** means *siblings (brothers and sisters)*. And again, even if there is only one male in the group, you still must use the masculine form.

And lastly, we know that a **niño** is a *boy*, and a **niña** is a *girl*. A group of *boys* would be **niños**, and a group of *girls* would be **niñas**. But what about a group of children that includes *boys* and *girls*? Again, even if there is only one boy, you would use the plural of the masculine form, which in this case would be **niños**. In Spanish, when the word **niños** is used, it often just means *children (girls and boys)*.

Of course, if you were involved in an actual conversation, you would know what the other person means because of the context of the conversation. However, in this book, since you are seeing these words in written form, the context is not always clear. Therefore, to help make things clearer, in the answer key we will occasionally put some brief explanatory notes in parentheses to reduce any possible confusion.

But before we leave this lesson, let's quickly review what we have learned:

WORD	POSSIBLE MEANINGS DEPENDING ON CONTEXT
amigos	• *friends* (male only) • *friends* (including males and females)
hermanos	• *brothers* • *siblings (brothers and sisters)*
niños	• *boys* • *children (boys and girls)*

LESSON 20

PLURAL ARTICLES

You already know about the articles **el** and **la**, which mean *the*. **El** and **la** are singular, and we use them with singular nouns. But what do you do if you want to put the word *the* in front of a plural noun?

If a noun is masculine and plural, and you want to put the word *the* in front of it, you would use the word **los**, as demonstrated in the following example:

Los muchachos *(the young men)*

If a noun is feminine and plural, we use the plural article **las**, as demonstrated in this example:

Las muchachas *(the young women)*

It may help you to study this handy chart:

	SINGULAR	PLURAL
MASCULINE	**el**	**los**
FEMININE	**la**	**las**

EXERCISES:

1. **Los muchachos**
2. **Las hermanas**
3. **Los amigos**
4. **Las muchachas**
5. **Los niños**
6. **Tu hermana y mi hermano**
7. **Una amiga**
8. **Los hermanos**
9. **Un amigo**
10. **La amiga**

Answers on 223.

LESSON 21

NEW WORDS **hombre / mujer**

MEANING *man / woman*

PRONUNCIATION TIP: In Spanish the letter *h* is always silent. So **hombre** sounds somewhat like *OHM-breh*. Also, in Spanish, the letter *j* sounds like the *h* in *hot*. So **mujer** sounds something like *moo-HERR*.

Mujer, which means *woman*, is the first noun that we have seen that ends with a consonant (in this case the letter *r*). So, to make **mujer** plural, we add **-es** to the end of the word, like this:

Mujer *(woman)* becomes **mujeres** *(women)*

The word **hombre** ends with a vowel, so to make it plural you would just add the letter *s* giving you **hombres**.

EXERCISES:

1. **Un hombre**
2. **Una mujer**
3. **El hombre y la mujer**
4. **Los hombres y las mujeres**
5. **Mi hermana y mi hermano**
6. **Tu amigo**
7. **Las muchachas**
8. **Los hombres**
9. **Las niñas**
10. **Mi amiga**

Answers on page 223.

22

LESSON 22

NEW WORDS   **mis / tus**

MEANING   *my* (plural) / *your* (plural)

We have already studied **mi** and **tu**, which are singular. But they both have plural forms, too.

The plural form of **mi** is **mis**. Use it with plural nouns, as in the following example:

Mis hermanos *(my brothers)*

And likewise, the plural form of **tu** is **tus**. Use it with plural nouns, as in the following example:

Tus hermanas *(your sisters)*

Mi, **tu**, **mis** and **tus** don't have masculine and feminine forms. They are always the same, no matter what the gender of the noun they are describing. ·

EXERCISES:

1. **Mis hermanos**
2. **Tus amigas**
3. **Mis niñas**
4. **Tus amigos**
5. **Un hombre y una mujer**
6. **Las muchachas y los muchachos**
7. **Mi hermana**
8. **Mis niños**
9. **El hombre y la mujer**
10. **Tu amigo**

Answers on page 223.

LESSON 23

NEW WORDS **hijo / hija**

MEANING *son / daughter*

PRONUNCIATION TIP: In Spanish the letter *h* is always silent. Also, in Spanish, the letter *j* sounds like the *h* in *hot*. So **hijo** sounds like *EEE-ho* and **hija** sounds like *EEE-ha*.

We have seen this before: the word **hijo** means *son*, and the word **hija** means *daughter*. A group of *sons* would be **hijos**, and a group of *daughters* would be **hijas**. But what about a group that includes someone's sons and daughters? As before, you would use the plural of the masculine form, which in this case would be **hijos**.

In Spanish, when the word **hijos** is used, it often just means *children*. But it is different from the word **niños**. While **niños** means *children* in the sense of *little boys and girls*, **hijos** means *children* in the sense of *offspring*.

EXERCISES:

1. **Mi hijo**
2. **Mis hijas**
3. **Tus hijos**
4. **Tu hija y mi hijo**
5. **Una hija y un hijo**
6. **Mi amiga**
7. **Un hombre y una mujer**
8. **Las muchachas y los muchachos**
9. **Mi hermano y tus hermanos**
10. **Tu hermano y mis amigos**

Answers on page 224.

LESSON 24

NEW WORDS **unos / unas**

MEANING *some* or *a few*

A while ago, we learned that the articles **el** and **la** were singular, and that they had the plural forms **los** and **las.**

Well, guess what? **Un** and **una** have plural forms, too. The plural form of **un** is **unos,** and the plural form of **una** is **unas.**

We already know that **un** and **una** mean *a* or *an.* But their plural forms, **unos** and **unas,** can mean *some* or *a few.* In the following examples, let's compare the use of **un** and **unos:**

> **Un hombre** *(a man)*
> **Unos hombres** *(some men)*

Now let's compare **una** and **unas:**

> **Una niña** *(a girl)*
> **Unas niñas** *(some girls)*

Here's a handy chart to help you remember these different forms:

	SINGULAR	PLURAL
MASCULINE	**un**	**unos**
FEMININE	**una**	**unas**

EXERCISES:

1. **Un hombre**
2. **Unos hombres**
3. **Una mujer**
4. **Unas mujeres**
5. **Las muchachas y los muchachos**
6. **Mi hermano**

7. **Unos niños**
8. **Tus amigos**
9. **Unas amigas**
10. **Mis hijas**

Answers on page 224.

LESSON 25

NEW WORDS **hola / adiós**

MEANING   *hello / goodbye*

PRONUNCIATION TIP: Remember that in Spanish, the letter *h* is always silent. So **hola** will sound like *OH-la*. Also, take note of the little mark over the letter *o* in **adiós**. That mark is called an *accent mark*, and it tells you which syllable of the word to emphasize or stress when you pronounce it.

In addition to **hola** and **adiós**, you should learn other common greetings such as **buenos días** *(good morning)*, **buenas tardes** *(good afternoon)* or **buenas noches** *(good evening* or *good night)*.

We have been including the gender in the answer key after the words **amigo** and **amiga**. But now that you have some experience working with these words, we will no longer put the gender of **amigo** and **amiga** in the answer key.

EXERCISES:

1. **Hola, amigo.**
2. **Adiós, mi amiga.**
3. **Buenos días, mis amigos.**
4. **Buenas tardes, amigos.**
5. **Buenas noches.**
6. **Unos muchachos y unas muchachas.**
7. **Mi hija y mi hijo.**
8. **Tus hijas.**
9. **Las muchachas.**
10. **El hombre.**

Answers on page 224.

LESSON 26

NEW WORDS   **padre / madre**

MEANING   *father / mother*

In addition to **padre** and **madre**, you should also know the less formal words for mother and father. **Papá** means *dad* and **mamá** means *mom*. Notice that in the words **papá** and **mamá** the accent mark is over the last syllable, so those words would be pronounced *ma-MAA* and *pa-PAA*.

Padres, the plural form of **padre**, usually just means *parents*.

EXERCISES:

1. **Hola, mamá.**
2. **Buenos días, papá.**
3. **Tus padres.**
4. **Buenas noches, padre.**
5. **Mis padres.**
6. **Buenas tardes, mi hija.**
7. **Un muchacho y una muchacha.**
8. **Adiós, mis amigos.**
9. **Buenas noches, mamá y papá.**
10. **Buenos días, madre.**

Answers on page 225.

LESSON 27

SUBJECTS AND VERBS

In any sentence, the two most important elements are the subject and the verb. Let's take a moment now to think about subjects and verbs.

In our very first lesson we learned that a *noun* is a person, place or thing. The subject of a sentence is the noun that is doing the action in the sentence. In each of the following examples, the underlined word is the subject of the sentence.

> <u>Matthew</u> kicked the ball.
> <u>Canada</u> is a large country.
> <u>Flowers</u> need sunshine.

Now let's talk about verbs. Verbs are words that tell us what the subject of the sentence is doing. Verbs can be action words such as *dance, shout, walk, talk* or *write*. Or, they can be verbs of being or existing such as *is, are, was, were,* and *will be*. Verbs of being are also called *linking verbs*. Let's look at those same sentences again, this time underlining the verb in each sentence.

> Matthew <u>kicked</u> the ball.
> Canada <u>is</u> a large country.
> Flowers <u>need</u> sunshine.

For practice, see if you can identify the subject and verb of each of the following sentences.

EXERCISES:

1. Kate walks to school every day.
2. My car is red.
3. My sister likes ice cream.
4. The horse is brown.
5. Harry told me a joke.
6. Last Thursday, Jim played softball.
7. Mark plays the trumpet.
8. My sister never cleans her room.
9. Julia loves bedtime stories.
10. The students are doing their homework.

Answers on page 225.

LESSON 28

PRONOUNS

A pronoun is a word that can take the place of a noun. Pronouns are words like *he, she, it, I, we, you* and *they*. We often use pronouns when we have already used a certain noun once and do not want to say that same noun again.

Here is an example of how we use pronouns in everyday speech.

Susanne is wearing a blue dress. <u>She</u> bought it last week.

Let's look at that last example again, this time without the word *she*.

Susanne is wearing a blue dress. <u>Susanne</u> bought it last week.

That example did not sound as good because the word *Susanne* was repeated. So you can see how useful pronouns can be in everyday conversation.

In each of the following exercises, try to identify the pronoun. And, if the pronoun is taking the place of another word, identify that word also.

EXERCISES:

1. Alfred's room is a mess because he never cleans up.
2. Jeff does not like going to the locker room because it is too smelly.
3. She already took out the trash.
4. The kids want to come inside because they are cold.
5. The teacher told Johnny to stop, but he didn't listen.
6. We are going to the beach.
7. They are not going to the party.
8. You are sitting in the wrong chair.
9. The rabbit was scared, so it ran away.
10. Don't disturb the children; they are asleep.

Answers on page 225.

LESSON 29

NEW WORDS **yo soy**

MEANING *I am*

PRONUNCIATION TIP: The pronunciation of **yo** can vary somewhat. It is common to hear a light *j* or *zh* sound at the beginning of the word **yo**. So you might hear it pronounced like *jo*, or like the *yo* in *yo-yo*.

This lesson is special because here we are learning our first Spanish verb. The word **yo** is a pronoun that means *I*, and **soy** is the verb.

Now that you know your first verb, we can make complete Spanish sentences for the first time.

EXERCISES:

1. **Yo soy tu madre.**
2. **Yo soy tu hermana.**
3. **Yo soy una niña.**
4. **Yo soy un muchacho.**
5. **Buenos días, mi amigo.**
6. **Hola, mamá; hola, papá.**
7. **Yo soy una muchacha.**
8. **Yo soy una mujer.**
9. **Adiós, hombres.**
10. **Buenas noches, mis amigos.**

Answers on page 226.

LESSON 30

NEW WORD **no**

MEANING *not*

The Spanish word **no** is like the English word *not.* **No** usually comes right before the verb, as seen in the following example:

Yo no soy tu hermano *(I am not your brother).*

This may seem strange at first, but you will get used to it with practice.

EXERCISES:

1. **Yo no soy una niña.**
2. **Yo no soy tu padre.**
3. **Yo no soy tu hermana.**
4. **Adiós, mis amigos.**
5. **Hola, papá.**
6. **Yo soy tu amiga.**
7. **Buenas tardes, mi hermano.**
8. **Yo no soy el hombre.**
9. **Buenos días, padre.**
10. **Hola, muchachos y muchachas.**

Answers on page 226.

LESSON 31

NEW WORDS **tú eres**

MEANING *you are*

Tú is the pronoun. It has an accent mark over the letter *u.* **Eres** is the verb. The other **tu** (the one that means *your)* does not have an accent mark over the letter *u.*

Tú eres is singular, so you would use it only when speaking to one person.

EXERCISES:

1. **Tú eres mi amiga.**
2. **Tú eres mi madre.**
3. **Tú no eres una niña.**
4. **Tú eres el muchacho.**
5. **Tú eres mi padre.**
6. **Tú eres una mujer.**
7. **Yo no soy tu hermana.**
8. **Buenas noches, mamá.**
9. **Yo soy tu hermano.**
10. **Tú eres mi hija.**

Answers on page 226.

LESSON 32

NEW WORDS   **él / ella**

MEANING   *he / she*

PRONUNCIATION TIP: The pronunciation of the *ll* in the middle of the word **ella** can vary somewhat. It is common to hear **ella** pronounced with a light *j* sound in the middle, like *EH-ja.* Or, you might hear **ella** pronounced with a *y* sound in the middle, like *EH-ya.*

At the beginning of this book, we learned that the word **el** means *the.* And that is still true. But the word **él** (notice the accent mark over the letter *e)* is the pronoun *he.* **Él** means *he,* and **ella** means *she.*

So when you are reading written Spanish, it's easy to distinguish **el** from **él** because of the accent mark. But in spoken Spanish, since **el** and **él** sound alike, the context of the sentence will help you understand what the speaker is saying.

In the next lesson, we will use **él** and **ella** in actual sentences.

LESSON 33

NEW WORD   **es**

MEANING   *is*

In the last lesson, you learned about the pronouns **él** and **ella**. Now you can use them with the verb **es**, which is the new word for this lesson.

EXERCISES:

1. **Él es mi padre.**
2. **Ella es mi madre.**
3. **Mi hermano es un niño.**
4. **Ella es tu hermana.**
5. **Ella es mi hija.**
6. **Yo soy tu amigo.**
7. **Tú eres mi papá.**
8. **Yo no soy una madre.**
9. **Tú no eres una mujer.**
10. **Yo soy una muchacha.**

Answers on page 227.

LESSON 34

FORMS OF ADDRESS

When talking to other people, we constantly use names and forms of address. If you know a person well, you will probably call him or her by his or her first name. But if it's a person you don't know very well, or someone older than you, you might refer to him or her by a form of address such as *Mr., Mrs.* or *Miss.* Or, you might say *sir* or *ma'am.*

In English, *Mr.* is a title given to adult men, whether married or not. *Mrs.* is used for married women, and *Miss* is used for unmarried women.

In Spanish, the word **señor** can mean either *Mr.* or *sir* depending on the context. Sometimes the word **señor** has an article in front of it, and sometimes not. Let's look at a few examples:

> **Hola, señor** *(Hello, sir).*
> **Hola, señor Smith** *(Hello, Mr. Smith).*

In those examples, it was not necessary to use an article in front of the word **señor**. This is because the speaker was speaking directly to Mr. Smith, using the word **señor** as a name by which to call Mr. Smith. But in other situations, you must use the article **el** in front of the word **señor**, as seen in these examples.

> **El señor Smith es mi amigo** *(Mr. Smith is my friend).*
> **Yo soy el señor Smith** *(I am Mr. Smith).*

In those last two examples it was necessary to use the article **el** in front of **señor** because the speaker was not using the word **señor** as a name by which to address a listener.

The word **señora** can mean either *Mrs.* or *Ma'am* depending on the context. In English, *Mrs.* is used for married women, but in Spanish, **señora** can be used for an older woman even if she is not married. Sometimes the word **señora** has an article in front of it, and sometimes not. Let's look at a few examples:

> **Buenos días, señora** *(Good morning, ma'am).*
> **Buenos días, señora Smith** *(Good morning, Mrs. Smith).*

In those examples, it was not necessary to use an article in front of the word **señora**. This is because the speaker was speaking directly to Mrs. Smith, using the word **señora** as a name by which to call Mrs. Smith. But in other situations, you must use the article **la** in front of the word **señora**, as seen in these examples.

> **La señora Smith es mi amiga** *(Mrs. Smith is my friend)*.
> **Yo soy la señora Smith** *(I am Mrs. Smith)*.

In those last two examples it was necessary to use the article **la** in front of **señora** because the speaker was not using the word **señora** as a name by which to address a listener.

Señorita means *miss*, or it can be used to address any woman who is not married. Sometimes the word **señorita** has an article in front of it, and sometimes not. Let's look at a few examples:

> **Buenos días, señorita** *(Good morning, Miss)*.
> **Buenos días, señorita Smith** *(Good morning, Miss Smith)*.

In those examples, it was not necessary to use an article in front of the word **señorita**. This is because the speaker was speaking directly to Miss Smith, using the word **señorita** as a name by which to call Miss Smith. But in other situations, you must use the article **la** in front of the word **señorita**, as seen in these examples.

> **La señorita Smith es mi amiga** *(Miss Smith is my friend)*.
> **Yo soy la señorita Smith** *(I am Miss Smith)*.

In those last two examples it was necessary to use the article **la** in front of **señorita** because the speaker was not using the word **señorita** as a name by which to address a listener.

EXERCISES:

1. **Buenos días, señor.**
2. **Buenos días, señor Jones.**
3. **El señor Jones es mi padre.**
4. **Él es mi padre.**
5. **Buenos días, señora.**
6. **Buenos días, señora Johnson.**
7. **La señora Johnson no es mi hermana.**
8. **Ella es mi hermana.**
9. **La señorita Smith es mi hija.**
10. **Ella es mi hija.**

Answers on page 227.

LESSON 35

NEW WORDS   **nosotros somos**

MEANING   *we are*

Nosotros is the pronoun here, and it means *we*. **Somos** is the verb.

Nosotros is the word you would use if the group of people being referred to is made up of only males or if it is a mixed group of males and females.

But if the group is made up of just females, then you would use the feminine form of **nosotros**, which is **nosotras**.

EXERCISES:

1. **Nosotros somos amigos.**
2. **Nosotras somos tus hermanas.**
3. **Nosotros no somos niños.**
4. **Buenos días, mis hijos.**
5. **Adiós, señora Smith.**
6. **Yo soy tu mamá.**
7. **Tú eres mi madre.**
8. **Él es mi amigo.**
9. **Ella es una muchacha.**
10. **Yo soy tu amiga.**

Answers on page 227.

LESSON 36

NEW WORDS   **vosotros sois**

MEANING   *you are* (plural)

You already know that **tú eres** means *you are*. We use **tú eres** when speaking to one person. **Vosotros sois** also means *you are*, but with one important difference: **vosotros sois** is plural. The English word *you* can refer to one person or more than one person. Other languages, such as Spanish, have different words for singular *you* and plural *you.*

Sometimes English speakers use expressions such as *you guys* or *you people* to try to make it clear that we are talking to more than one person. In the southeastern United States, we often use the contraction *y'all* to address more than one person (never just one). *Y'all* is simply a contraction of the words *you* and *all. Y'all* rhymes with *hall, ball* and *fall.*

So, in the answer key, **vosotros sois** will be translated as *y'all are*, to help you distinguish plural *you* from singular *you.* If you are from the southeastern United States, using this word will be easy for you. If not, y'all will get used to it after using it a few times. In any case, just try to have fun with it.

The pronoun **vosotros** is used only in Spain, not in the Americas (some Spanish books don't tell you that). In Latin America, they have a different way of saying the plural *you* which we will tell you about later in the book.

Oops! We almost forgot. There is a feminine form of **vosotros** too, and that is the word **vosotras**. That would be used if addressing a group of females only. If it's a group of males, or a mixed group of males and females, you would use **vosotros**.

EXERCISES:

1. **Vosotros sois mis amigos.**
2. **Vosotros sois mis hijos.**
3. **Vosotras sois hermanas.**
4. **Buenas tardes, mi amigo.**
5. **Él es mi papá.**
6. **El señor Smith es mi hermano.**
7. **Adiós, señor Smith.**

8. **Nosotras no somos niñas.**
9. **Tú no eres mi hermano.**
10. **Ella es mi amiga.**

Answers on page 228.

LESSON 37

NEW WORDS **ellos / ellas**

MEANING *they*

PRONUNCIATION TIP: The pronunciation of the *ll* in the middle of the words **ellos** and **ellas** can vary somewhat. It is common to hear these words pronounced with a light *j* sound in the middle, or with a *y* sound in the middle.

Ellos is the plural form of the masculine pronoun **él**. And likewise, **ellas** is the plural form of **ella**. **Ellos** and **ellas** both mean *they*.

If you want to say *they* (referring to a group of males) you would use the word **ellos**. If you want to say *they* (referring to a group of females only) you would use the word **ellas**. If the group of people contains both males and females, you would use **ellos**, the masculine form.

LESSON 38

NEW WORD **son**

MEANING *are*

In the last lesson, you learned about the pronouns **ellos** and **ellas**. Now you can use them with the verb **son**, the new word for this lesson, which means *are*.

EXERCISES:

1. **Ellos son mis hermanos.**
2. **Ellos son mis amigos.**
3. **Ellas son mis hijas.**
4. **Vosotras sois mis amigas.**
5. **Nosotros somos hombres.**
6. **Buenos días, señor Jones.**
7. **Las mujeres son mis hermanas.**
8. **Ella es mi mamá.**
9. **Tú eres un muchacho.**
10. **Nosotros somos amigos.**

Answers on page 228.

LESSON 39

MEMORIZATION

Let's put all the pronouns and verbs you know into a chart to help you remember them.

yo soy	**nosotros/nosotras somos**
tú eres	**vosotros/vosotras sois**
él/ella es	**ellos/ellas son**

When studying any language, it is very beneficial to memorize groups of verbs such as the one you see here. Of course, the most common way to memorize these verbs is simply to repeat them over and over. This might be a little boring, but you can make this necessary repetition more fun by making a song or a game out of it, especially if children are involved.

LESSON 40

PERSON

We have already covered singular and plural. Now let's talk about another quality that verbs have. In Spanish, verbs (with help from their pronouns) tell not only what action is taking place, but also who is performing the action. Verbs can be in the first person, second person, or third person.

- ❑ Verbs that refer to *I* or *we* are first person (the person who is speaking).

- ❑ Verbs that refer to *you*, either singular or plural, are second person (the person or people to whom the speaker is speaking). In this book we will use *y'all* for the second person plural to help distinguish it from the second person singular.

- ❑ Verbs that refer to *he, she, it*, or *they* are third person (the person, thing, people, or things being spoken about).

The following chart should help illustrate this concept:

	SINGULAR	PLURAL
FIRST PERSON	I	we
SECOND PERSON	you	you
THIRD PERSON	he, she, it	they

y'all

In the exercises on the next page, determine what the subject of each sentence is. Then, determine if it is first person, second person, or third person. Finally, determine whether it is singular or plural.

EXERCISES:

1. I am tired.
2. You are really good at chess.
3. She passed the test.
4. We are going to school.
5. Y'all have an expensive car.
6. They eat breakfast at Aunt Martha's house every Saturday.
7. He is a trombone player.
8. It is a history book.
9. Y'all really know how to throw a party.
10. The flowers in your garden are very colorful.

Answers on page 228.

LESSON 41

Now let's put all the Spanish verbs you know into a chart.

	SINGULAR	PLURAL
FIRST PERSON	**yo soy**	**nosotros/nosotras somos**
SECOND PERSON	**tú eres**	**vosotros/vosotras sois** (Spain only)
THIRD PERSON	**él/ella es**	**ellos/ellas son**

Try to memorize all these forms. As you think of each form, try also to think about what it means.

LESSON 42

NUMBERS

In this lesson, let's try to memorize the numbers *one* through *six* in Spanish. Here is a chart to help you learn these numbers.

English	Spanish
zero	**cero**
one	**uno**
two	**dos**
three	**tres**
four	**cuatro**
five	**cinco**
six	**seis**

You would only use the word **uno** if counting or talking about numbers, such as doing math or giving someone your phone number.

If you want to say *one man* or *one* of something you would still just use the article **un** or **una**.

EXERCISES:

1. **Un hombre.**
2. **Una hermana.**
3. **552-4106 (cinco cinco dos cuatro uno cero seis).**
4. **Dos mujeres.**
5. **Tres hijos.**
6. **Cinco mujeres.**
7. **Seis hombres y cuatro mujeres.**
8. **Ellos son mis hermanos.**
9. **Nosotros somos tus padres.**
10. **Él es mi padre.**

Answers on page 229.

L E S S O N   4 3

NUMBERS, CONTINUED

In this lesson, let's try to memorize the numbers *seven* through *twelve* in Spanish.

English	Spanish
seven	**siete**
eight	**ocho**
nine	**nueve**
ten	**diez**
eleven	**once**
twelve	**doce**

Here are some exercises to help you learn to translate these numbers.

EXERCISES:

1. **Siete muchachas.**
2. **Ocho niños.**
3. **898-0417 (ocho nueve ocho cero cuatro uno siete).**
4. **Diez padres.**
5. **Once amigos.**
6. **Doce hijos.**
7. **Tú eres mi amiga.**
8. **La señorita Smith no es mi hermana.**
9. **Mi madre es la señora Jones.**
10. **Ellos son mis amigos.**

Answers on page 229.

LESSON 44

NEW WORDS **perro / gato**

MEANING *dog / cat*

PRONUNCIATION TIP: When you say **perro**, be sure to roll the *r* sound.

Perro and **gato** are masculine nouns. However, you might also see the word **perra** used to refer to a *female dog*, and the word **gata** used to refer to a *female cat*.

EXERCISES:

1. **Cinco gatos.**
2. **Cuatro perros.**
3. **Tres hermanos y dos hermanas.**
4. **Seis gatos y nueve perros.**
5. **Siete amigas.**
6. **Mis perros y mi gata.**
7. **Once niños.**
8. **Ellas son mis hijas.**
9. **Yo soy tu amiga.**
10. **Hola, mis niños.**

Answers on page 229.

LESSON 45

NEW WORDS **yo tengo**

MEANING *I have*

Yo tengo is our first action verb in Spanish. All the verbs you have learned so far have been verbs of being or existing (also known as linking verbs). But now that we know how to say **yo tengo**, hopefully we can make more interesting sentences!

EXERCISES:

1. **Yo tengo un gato.**
2. **Yo tengo dos perras.**
3. **Yo tengo diez gatos y un perro.**
4. **Yo tengo unos gatos.**
5. **Tú eres mi hija.**
6. **Tu hermana es mi hermana.**
7. **Yo tengo un hijo.**
8. **Ella es mi hermana.**
9. **Yo tengo los perros.**
10. **El señor Smith es mi amigo.**

Answers on page 230.

LESSON 46

NEW WORD **también**

MEANING *also*

EXERCISES:

1. **Yo tengo ocho perros y también un gato.**
2. **Yo tengo cuatro hermanos y también tres hermanas.**
3. **Yo tengo doce gatos.**
4. **Yo no tengo una hija.**
5. **Buenos días, señorita.**
6. **Mi perro es mi amigo.**
7. **Hola, señora Smith.**
8. **La señora Jones es mi mamá.**
9. **Yo tengo unos perros y unos gatos también.**
10. **Yo soy una mujer.**

Answers on page 230.

LESSON 47

NEW WORD **dinero**

MEANING *money*

The word **dinero** is masculine, as are most nouns that end with **–o**.

EXERCISES:

1. **Yo tengo dinero.**
2. **Yo no tengo dinero.**
3. **Yo no tengo tu dinero.**
4. **Ellas son mis hermanas.**
5. **Nosotras somos amigas.**
6. **Yo tengo unos gatos y también un perro.**
7. **Buenas noches, señor.**
8. **Yo tengo tres niños.**
9. **Tu hermana es mi amiga.**
10. **Adiós, señorita Smith.**

Answers on page 230.

LESSON 48

NEW WORD **dólar**

MEANING *dollar*

PRONUNCIATION TIP: In the word **dólar**, the accent goes on the first syllable.

The word **dólar** is masculine.

EXERCISES:

1. **Yo tengo un dólar.**
2. **Yo tengo diez dólares.**
3. **Yo tengo cuatro dólares.**
4. **Yo tengo dinero.**
5. **Yo tengo siete gatos y también un perro.**
6. **Buenas tardes, señorita.**
7. **Las niñas son mis hijas.**
8. **Mis padres son el señor Smith y la señora Smith.**
9. **Ella es mi hija.**
10. **La señora Jones es mi amiga.**

Answers on page 231.

LESSON 49

NEW WORDS   **tú tienes**

MEANING   *you have*

This chart should come in handy as we learn all the different forms of **yo tengo**.

	SINGULAR	PLURAL
FIRST PERSON	**yo tengo**	
SECOND PERSON	**tú tienes**	
THIRD PERSON		

EXERCISES:

1. **Tú tienes mi dinero.**
2. **Tú tienes nueve perros y también un gato.**
3. **Tú tienes mi perro.**
4. **Yo no tengo tu dinero.**
5. **Yo no soy un padre.**
6. **Mi perro es mi amigo.**
7. **Tú tienes ocho dólares.**
8. **El señor Smith es mi padre.**
9. **Adiós, madre.**
10. **Nosotros no somos hermanos.**

Answers on page 231.

L E S S O N   5 0

NEW WORDS   **él tiene / ella tiene**

MEANING   *he has / she has*

The chart is getting fuller:

	SINGULAR	PLURAL
FIRST PERSON	**yo tengo**	
SECOND PERSON	**tú tienes**	
THIRD PERSON	**él/ella tiene**	

EXERCISES:

1. **Él tiene un perro.**
2. **Ella tiene un gato.**
3. **Él no tiene dinero.**
4. **Ella tiene seis dólares.**
5. **Él tiene cuatro niños.**
6. **Adiós, mis amigos.**
7. **Tú tienes dos hermanas y también un hermano.**
8. **Yo tengo siete dólares.**
9. **Ellos son mis amigos.**
10. **Nosotros no somos niños.**

Answers on page 231.

LESSON 51

NEW WORD **pero**

MEANING *but*

Honestly, we are not trying to confuse you, but…

PRONUNCIATION TIP: You already know the word **perro**, which means *dog*. But **pero**, the new word for this lesson, has only one *r*. These two words sound somewhat similar, but the word **perro** has a longer rolled *r* sound than **pero**.

Listen carefully to the pronunciation recordings and you will hear this subtle difference in pronunciation. Then, try to make your pronunciation sound just like the recording.

EXERCISES:

1. **Yo no tengo una hermana, pero tú tienes tres hermanas.**
2. **Él no tiene dinero, pero ella tiene once dólares.**
3. **Tú no tienes un gato, pero ella tiene siete gatos.**
4. **Mi gato es mi amigo.**
5. **El señor Jones es mi padre y la señora Jones es mi madre.**
6. **Nosotras somos amigas.**
7. **Buenos días, señorita.**
8. **Yo tengo cuatro perros y también un gato.**
9. **Las muchachas son mis amigas.**
10. **Yo tengo unas amigas.**

Answers on page 232.

LESSON 52

NEW WORDS   **nosotros / nosotras tenemos**

MEANING   *we have*

We're over halfway there!

	SINGULAR	PLURAL
FIRST PERSON	**yo tengo**	**nosotros/nosotras tenemos**
SECOND PERSON	**tú tienes**	
THIRD PERSON	**él/ella tiene**	

EXERCISES:

1. **Nosotros tenemos amigos.**
2. **Nosotros no tenemos dinero, pero tú tienes cinco dólares.**
3. **Nosotras tenemos dos hermanas.**
4. **Tú tienes un dólar.**
5. **La señora Smith es mi madre.**
6. **Ella tiene cinco hijos y dos hijas.**
7. **Las niñas son mis hermanas.**
8. **Tú tienes ocho dólares.**
9. **Tú eres mi amigo, pero él es mi hermano.**
10. **Ella tiene un hermano y también una hermana.**

Answers on page 232.

LESSON 53

NEW WORDS   **vosotros / vosotras tenéis**

MEANING   *y'all have*

The chart is almost full now—please try to contain your excitement.

Remember that **vosotros/vosotras tenéis** is used only in Spain, not in the Americas.

	SINGULAR	PLURAL
FIRST PERSON	**yo tengo**	**nosotros/nosotras tenemos**
SECOND PERSON	**tú tienes**	**vosotros/vosotras tenéis**
THIRD PERSON	**él/ella tiene**	

EXERCISES:

1. **Vosotros tenéis tres perros.**
2. **Vosotros no tenéis dinero.**
3. **Vosotros no tenéis dinero, pero nosotros tenemos nueve dólares.**
4. **Vosotras tenéis seis dólares.**
5. **El hombre tiene un gato y un perro.**
6. **Él no es mi amigo.**
7. **Ellas son mis amigas.**
8. **El hombre no tiene un gato, pero la mujer tiene cuatro gatos.**
9. **Los niños son tus hermanos y tus hermanas.**
10. **Tú tienes siete hermanas.**

Answers on page 232.

LESSON 54

NEW WORDS **ellos / ellas tienen**

MEANING *they have*

Our chart is now full!

	Singular	Plural
First Person	**yo tengo**	**nosotros/nosotras tenemos**
Second Person	**tú tienes**	**vosotros/vosotras tenéis** (Spain only)
Third Person	**él/ella tiene**	**ellos/ellas tienen**

EXERCISES:

1. **Ellos tienen doce dólares.**
2. **Ellas tienen tres hermanas.**
3. **Ellos tienen dos niños, pero nosotros no tenemos niños.**
4. **Tú no tienes un hermano, pero yo tengo dos hermanas.**
5. **Yo tengo cuatro gatos y también unos perros.**
6. **Tú eres mi amigo.**
7. **Mis padres son mis amigos.**
8. **Buenas noches, mis amigos.**
9. **Los muchachos son mis hijos.**
10. **El señor Smith tiene tres hijos.**

Answers on page 233.

LESSON 55

We now know all the present tense forms of **yo soy** and **yo tengo**. Let's review them now. Here is the chart for **yo soy**:

	SINGULAR	PLURAL
FIRST PERSON	**yo soy**	**nosotros/nosotras somos**
SECOND PERSON	**tú eres**	**vosotros/vosotras sois** (Spain only)
THIRD PERSON	**él/ella es**	**ellos/ellas son**

You should make every effort to memorize these forms. Chant them. Sing them. Do whatever helps you to memorize the different verb forms.

Here is the chart for **yo tengo**:

	SINGULAR	PLURAL
FIRST PERSON	**yo tengo**	**nosotros/nosotras tenemos**
SECOND PERSON	**tú tienes**	**vosotros/vosotras tenéis** (Spain only)
THIRD PERSON	**él/ella tiene**	**ellos/ellas tienen**

As you repeat or recite these verb forms, try to think of what each word means as you say it. In the next few lessons, we will learn more about Spanish verbs and how they function.

LESSON 56

STEMS AND PERSONAL ENDINGS

You may have noticed by now that there is a pattern to the endings of Spanish verbs. For instance, the first person plural verbs always end in **–mos**, as seen in words like **somos** and **tenemos**. Also, the second person singular verbs always end in **–s**, as seen in words like **eres** and **tienes**.

Let's take a closer look at the verb **yo tengo** for a moment. Each form of **yo tengo** starts with either **teng-, tien-,** or **ten-**. That part of the verb is called the *stem*. We will learn more about verb stems later in the book.

After the stem, each different form of the verb has its own special, individual ending. If we isolated those endings and put them into a chart, the chart would look like this:

	SINGULAR	PLURAL
FIRST PERSON	**-o**	**-emos**
SECOND PERSON	**-es**	**-éis**
THIRD PERSON	**-e**	**-en**

We will call these special endings *personal endings*. They show whether a verb is first person, second person or third person, and whether the verb is singular or plural.

When you understand how verb stems and personal endings work, it's much easier to understand and use Spanish verbs. There are certain rules to follow, and patterns to learn, too. Throughout the rest of this book, we will study these rules and patterns and gain a deeper understanding of how the Spanish verb system works.

LESSON 57

WHY DOES SPANISH HAVE PERSONAL ENDINGS?

In the last lesson, we learned about six special verb endings called *personal endings*. These personal endings indicate whether a verb is first person, second person or third person, and whether the verb is singular or plural. But why do Spanish verbs have these personal endings in the first place?

Well, to make a long story short, the Spanish language is a direct descendant of Latin, the language of the ancient Romans. When the Romans conquered and occupied other countries, they brought their language, Latin, with them. So for a long time, Latin was spoken throughout a large part of Europe. But later, after the fall of the Roman empire, the Latin that was spoken in places like Spain, France and Italy gradually changed into Spanish, French and Italian. That's why many Spanish words are so closely related to Latin words. Not only is the entire Spanish verb system derived from Latin, but much of the vocabulary, too.

Here's an example: In Latin, **sumus** means *we are*. Over time, the vowels in **sumus** changed from *u* sounds to *o* sounds, and it became the Spanish word **somos**.

Another example: In Latin, **mulier** means *woman*. Over time, the *l* sound in **mulier** softened to an *h* sound, and became the Spanish word **mujer**.

Just for fun, see if you can match the original Latin word on the left with the Spanish word that came from it on the right.

rex *(king)*	**verdad**
exercitus *(army)*	**rey**
homo *(man)*	**estrella**
terra *(land)*	**árbol**
veritas *(truth)*	**hombre**
octo *(eight)*	**tierra**
arbor *(tree)*	**ocho**
stella *(star)*	**ejército**

Answers on page 233.

LESSON 58

NEW WORD **su**

MEANING *his, her*

You already know how to say *my* and *your,* but in this lesson we are going to learn how to say *his* and *her.* For this, we use the word **su.**

If we put **mi**, **tu**, and **su** into a chart, it would look like this.

	SINGULAR
FIRST PERSON	**mi**
SECOND PERSON	**tu**
THIRD PERSON	**su**

You see, **mi** *(my)* makes reference to the speaker, so it is first person. **Tu** *(your)* makes reference to the person being spoken to, so it is second person. And **su**, our new word for this lesson, refers to the person being spoken about, so it is third person. In this book, we will limit our study of these words to the singular forms which you see in the chart above. In other words, we will not study how to say *our, their,* or (GULP) *y'all's.*

Let's study some examples with the word **su.**

> **El hombre tiene su dinero** *(The man has his money).*
> **La mujer tiene su perro** *(The woman has her dog).*

Here's a rule to remember: If a noun is singular, then any word that modifies that noun (such as an adjective) must also be singular. And likewise, if a noun is plural, any word that modifies that noun (such as an adjective) must be plural.

So when it comes to the word **su**, if the thing being possessed is plural, use the plural form of **su** which is **sus.** Here is an example of a sentence with **sus.**

> **La mujer tiene sus perros** *(The woman has her dogs).*

Notice that **su** can mean *his* or *her*. It covers both genders. In a conversation, you must rely on the context of the conversation to know whom the speaker is talking about. In our exercises, we will try to provide sufficient context so that you will know if **su** means *his* or *her*.

EXERCISES:

1. **La madre tiene su niño.**
2. **Mi hermano tiene su dinero.**
3. **Mi amigo tiene sus perros, pero yo no tengo mi perro.**
4. **Nosotros tenemos cuatro hermanos.**
5. **Los niños tienen un gato.**
6. **Tú eres mi amigo.**
7. **Ella tiene siete dólares.**
8. **Mis padres tienen once hijos.**
9. **Yo tengo unos perros y también un gato.**
10. **Adiós, papá.**

Answers on page 233.

LESSON 59

SHOWING POSSESSION

Possessive words show ownership of something. In English, we often show possession by using an apostrophe followed by the letter *s*. Consider the following examples:

> Fred's car
> The nation's flag
> Arizona's capital

Sometimes we show possession by using the word *of*.

> The peak of the mountain
> The smell of garlic
> The beginning of the show

So in English, when you want to show possession of something, you must decide whether to use an apostrophe or the word *of*.

Here are a few of the most basic rules to remember when using apostrophes:

	RULE	EXAMPLE
RULE #1	To make a noun that does not end in *s* possessive, just add an apostrophe and an *s*.	Lauren always wants to borrow Kate's Spanish book.
RULE #2	To make a singular noun that ends in *s* possessive, add an apostrophe and an *s* (just like rule #1).	The class's favorite subject was Spanish.
RULE #3	To make a plural noun that ends in *s* possessive, add an apostrophe to the end of the word.	Due to increased interest in Spanish, all the books' covers are starting to wear out.

LESSON 60

SHOWING POSSESSION IN SPANISH

In the last lesson, we learned that to show possession in English, we may use either an apostrophe and the letter *s* or the word *of*. So in English, there are two ways to show possession.

In Spanish, however, there is only one way, and that is to use the word *of* which in Spanish is **de**. The word **de** is placed directly after the thing that is being possessed, as seen in the following sentence:

> **El perro de mi padre** *(my father's dog)*

If you translated it word for word, it would say *The dog of my father*. But a better, smoother translation would be *My father's dog*. Here's another example:

> **El gato de la mujer** *(the woman's cat)*

Again, in this example, if you translated it word for word, it would say *The cat of the woman*. But again, it is better and smoother to translate it as *The woman's cat*.

EXERCISES:

1. **La amiga de la mujer.**
2. **La hermana de mi madre.**
3. **El perro de mi hermana.**
4. **El dinero de mis padres.**
5. **Ellos tienen tres dólares, pero yo no tengo dinero.**
6. **Mis niños tienen cinco dólares.**
7. **Los muchachos tienen dinero.**
8. **Mi amigo tiene cuatro perros.**
9. **Yo soy una niña.**
10. **El hombre tiene su dinero.**

Answers on page 234

L E S S O N 61

MORE ABOUT DE

There is one more thing we need to tell you about the word **de**. If the word **de** comes before the word **el**, then **de** and **el** must be smashed together to form the word **del**. So if you have a sentence like this:

El dinero <u>de el</u> hombre *(the man's money)*

You would take the words **de** and **el** and smash them together into the word **del**, like this:

El dinero <u>del</u> hombre *(the man's money)*

So remember this formula: **de + el = del.**

EXERCISES:

1. **Los niños del hombre.**
2. **La hermana del muchacho.**
3. **Los amigos del niño.**
4. **Yo no tengo el dinero del muchacho.**
5. **Nosotros no tenemos el perro de la mujer.**
6. **Ellos tienen seis niños, dos gatos y un perro.**
7. **Mi madre tiene diez dólares, pero mi padre no tiene su dinero.**
8. **Ella tiene el dinero de sus padres.**
9. **Nosotros no tenemos un gato.**
10. **Nosotros somos tus padres.**

Answers on page 234

LESSON 62

NEW WORD **carro**

MEANING *car*

PRONUNCIATION TIP: Roll the *r* sound in the middle of the word **carro**.

Carro is a masculine noun, so it will need a masculine article like **el** or **un**.

EXERCISES:

1. **El carro de mi hermana.**
2. **Yo tengo el carro de mi papá.**
3. **El dinero del hombre.**
4. **El carro de mi amigo.**
5. **El gato del hombre.**
6. **Mi hermano tiene su carro.**
7. **Tú no tienes un carro.**
8. **Nosotros tenemos ocho dólares, pero tú no tienes dinero.**
9. **Buenas noches, señor Jones.**
10. **Ella tiene el carro de su madre y también su dinero.**

Answers on page 234.

LESSON 63

LEAVING OUT THE PRONOUN

So far, whenever we have used verbs, we have always used pronouns along with the verbs, like this:

Yo soy *(I am).*

In that example, **yo** is the pronoun and **soy** is the verb. But in Spanish, sometimes the pronoun gets left out completely, as in this example:

Soy *(I am).*

So the word **soy** means *I am* by itself, even without the word **yo**.

A Spanish speaker will usually include the pronoun in order to be specific—that is, to show clearly who the subject of the sentence is. Usually a Spanish speaker will only omit the pronoun if it is very clear who the subject of the sentence is. Let's demonstrate this with an example:

Yo no tengo un hermano, pero tengo una hermana *(I do not have a brother, but I have a sister).*

In the first part of that sentence, the speaker included the pronoun **yo** to demonstrate clearly that the person speaking was the subject of the sentence. But in the second part of the sentence, since it was obvious that the speaker was referring to himself, there was no need to repeat the pronoun, so the speaker left it out. So the word **yo** is used for emphasis.

In a real Spanish conversation, everyone participating in the conversation might know from the context who the speaker is talking about. So there are many situations in which the speaker might leave out the pronoun.

In the following exercises, we have provided some sentences where the pronoun is omitted so you can practice this concept.

EXERCISES:

1. **Yo tengo un perro.**
2. **Tengo un perro.**
3. **Tú tienes un gato.**
4. **Tienes un gato.**
5. **Él no tiene un hermano, pero tiene dos hermanas.**
6. **Nosotras somos amigas.**
7. **Somos amigas.**
8. **Soy un hombre.**
9. **Mi padre no tiene su carro, pero tiene su dinero.**
10. **Ellos tienen el gato de mi mamá.**

Answers on page 235.

LESSON 64

IDIOMS

In conversation, we often use sayings and expressions that carry a meaning other than what the words mean when taken literally. We call these expressions *idioms*.

An idiom could be a saying like this: *I'm still sitting on the fence.* If you say that you are sitting on the fence, it does not mean that you are actually sitting on top of a fence—instead it means that you have not made up your mind about something. So certain expressions and sayings like that could be called idioms.

Other times, we use the term *idiom* to describe phrases in another language that are not translated into English literally. For instance, a phrase commonly found in another language might be worded much differently than that same phrase would be worded in the English language. So when we translate a Spanish idiom into English, we will not keep the original Spanish wording. Instead, we will translate the meaning of the idiom into English the way an English speaker would normally say it.

LESSON 65

NEW IDIOM **yo tengo hambre**

MEANING *I am hungry*

In this lesson, we will learn our first Spanish idiom. It concerns one of the authors' favorite subjects: *food.*

In English, we say *I am hungry.* But in Spanish, this would be worded a bit differently. This is how you say *I am hungry* in Spanish:

> **Yo tengo hambre.**

Tengo, as you already know, means *I have.* And the word **hambre** means *hunger.* So literally, **yo tengo hambre** means *I have hunger.* But as an idiom, we translate it into English as *I am hungry.*

If you want to say *I am thirsty*, the situation is exactly the same:

> **Yo tengo sed.**

The word **sed** means *thirst.* So literally, **yo tengo sed** means *I have thirst.* But as an idiom, we translate it into English as *I am thirsty.*

Don't forget that sometimes the pronoun is omitted, so you might see sentences like this:

> **Tengo hambre.**
> **Tengo sed.**

If someone else is hungry or thirsty, just use the different forms of **tengo** along with **hambre** or **sed**, as shown in these examples:

> **Él tiene hambre** *(He is hungry).*
> **Nosotros tenemos sed** *(We are thirsty).*

It is now time for the authors' afternoon snack, so while we get some food, translate these exercises.

EXERCISES:

1. **Yo tengo hambre.**
2. **Tengo hambre.**
3. **Yo tengo sed.**
4. **Tengo sed.**
5. **Mi perro tiene hambre.**
6. **Ellas tienen sed.**
7. **Tú no tienes un carro.**
8. **Nosotros no tenemos un gato, pero tenemos un perro.**
9. **Mi hijo tiene el carro del hombre.**
10. **Tu amigo tiene su perro.**

Answers on page 235.

LESSON 66

NEW WORDS **yo quiero**

MEANING *I want*

When we learned about **yo tengo**, we learned each form one at a time. But now that you have some experience working with verbs, there is no need to learn every new verb one form at a time. So in this lesson, we are going to give you all the forms of **yo quiero** at the same time. But before we do, let's review the personal endings that we learned a few lessons ago.

	SINGULAR	PLURAL
FIRST PERSON	**-o**	**-emos**
SECOND PERSON	**-es**	**-éis**
THIRD PERSON	**-e**	**-en**

So here are the different forms of **yo quiero**.

	SINGULAR	PLURAL
FIRST PERSON	**yo quiero**	**nosotros/nosotras queremos**
SECOND PERSON	**tú quieres**	**vosotros/vosotras queréis** (Spain only)
THIRD PERSON	**él/ella quiere**	**ellos/ellas quieren**

In the next lesson, we will learn more about the verb **yo quiero**. But in the meantime, try to memorize the different forms of **yo quiero** as best you can, and then try the exercises.

74

EXERCISES:

1. **Papá, yo quiero un gato.**
2. **Él quiere diez dólares.**
3. **Nosotras queremos un carro.**
4. **Tú quieres cinco dólares.**
5. **Ellas quieren el perro de mi hermano.**
6. **Mi hermana tiene un perro.**
7. **Mi perro tiene hambre.**
8. **Yo tengo sed, pero tú no tienes sed.**
9. **Mi hermana tiene doce dólares.**
10. **Ellos quieren el dinero de mi papá.**

Answers on page 235.

LESSON 67

MORE ABOUT VERB STEMS

So far, we have been paying a lot of attention to the personal endings of verbs, but we have only briefly mentioned verb stems. So in this lesson, we would like to examine verb stems a bit more, using **yo quiero** as an example.

First, let's review the forms of **yo quiero** that we learned in the last lesson.

	SINGULAR	PLURAL
FIRST PERSON	**yo quiero**	**nosotros/nosotras queremos**
SECOND PERSON	**tú quieres**	**vosotros/vosotras queréis** (Spain only)
THIRD PERSON	**él/ella quiere**	**ellos/ellas quieren**

In Spanish, some verbs have the same stem for every form of the verb. We call these verbs *regular verbs* because their forms are regular and predictable.

But that's not the case with **yo quiero**. If we took just the stem of each form of **yo quiero**, it would look like the chart you see below. What observations can you make about these stems?

	SINGULAR	PLURAL
FIRST PERSON	**quier-**	**quer-**
SECOND PERSON	**quier-**	**quer-**
THIRD PERSON	**quier-**	**quier-**

76

This verb is supposed to be based on a **quer-** stem (you will learn more about this later). But a close examination of the chart shows that only two of the forms are based on the **quer-** stem, while in the other forms, the stem changes to **quier-**. So instead of just having the letter *e* in the middle of the stem, these forms have *ie* instead.

So when you look at the different forms of **yo quiero**, notice that in the first person singular, second person singular, third person singular, and third person plural, the stem changes to **quier-**. Those forms are circled in the chart below.

	SINGULAR	PLURAL
FIRST PERSON	quiero	queremos
SECOND PERSON	quieres	queréis
THIRD PERSON	quiere	quieren

Yo quiero and other verbs like it are called *stem-changing verbs* because in the first person singular, second person singular, third person singular, and third person plural, the stem changes from what it is supposed to be.

Give this some thought, and in the next lesson we will learn more about stem-changing verbs.

LESSON 68

SHOE VERBS

In the last lesson we learned about a special kind of Spanish verb called a *stem-changing verb*. With a stem-changing verb, the stem is what it ought to be for the first person plural and second person plural, but the stem changes in all the other forms.

But there is another name for these verbs that is much more fun: *shoe verbs.* Now you may be asking, "Why on earth are they called *shoe verbs*?" Well, here's the reason: If you made a chart with the different forms of **yo quiero**, and drew a shape around the forms that have the changed stem, that shape would look something like a shoe.

To demonstrate this, we decided to hire a talented artist to create the perfect shoe verb chart (actually, the artist made it look more like a roller skate).

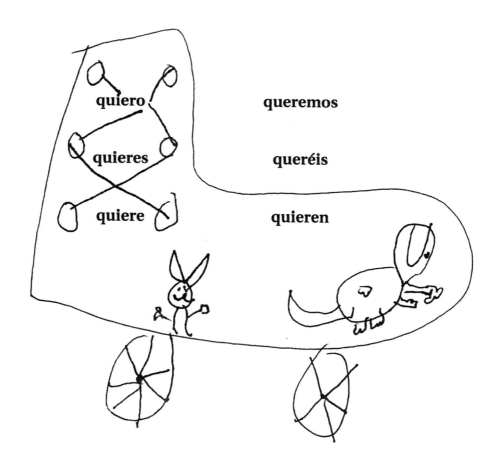

LESSON 69

DRAW YOUR OWN SHOE

In the last lesson, we learned about shoe verbs, and we even saw an example of a shoe verb chart with the shoe drawn in. Well, it wasn't exactly a shoe, it was more of a roller skate (with some animals on it just for decoration).

But we wanted to give you a chance to draw your own shoe, too. So, take a look at the verb chart below, and see if you can "shoe" us your artistic abilities by drawing a shoe around the forms of **yo quiero** that are based on the **quier-** stem, while leaving the **quer-** forms outside of the shoe.

quiero	**queremos**
quieres	**queréis**
quiere	**quieren**

LESSON 70

NEW WORD **comida**

MEANING *food*

PRONUNCIATION TIP: In the word comida, the accent is on the middle syllable. So **comida** sounds like *ko-MEE-dah*.

Comida is a feminine noun, so it will need a feminine article such as **la** or **una**.

EXERCISES:

1. **Ellas quieren comida.**
2. **Nosotros tenemos hambre, pero no tenemos comida.**
3. **Mi papá quiere comida.**
4. **Los gatos tienen hambre.**
5. **Ellos tienen hambre, pero no tienen dinero.**
6. **Ellos quieren un gato y unos perros.**
7. **Nosotras tenemos el carro.**
8. **El perro quiere la comida del gato.**
9. **Mis niños quieren mi dinero.**
10. **La señora Jones quiere dinero también.**

Answers on page 236.

LESSON 71

NEW WORD **porque**

MEANING *because*

PRONUNCIATION TIP: In the word **porque**, the accent goes on the first syllable. So it sounds similar to *PORE-keh*. If you put the accent on the second syllable, the meaning of the word changes (so don't do that).

EXERCISES:

1. **Tú quieres comida porque tienes hambre.**
2. **Yo no tengo un carro porque no tengo dinero.**
3. **Nosotros tenemos hambre, pero no tenemos comida.**
4. **Mi amigo quiere un perro.**
5. **Mi padre no tiene su perro.**
6. **Mis amigos tienen sed.**
7. **Los niños tienen siete dólares.**
8. **Yo tengo un perro.**
9. **Nosotros queremos comida porque tenemos hambre.**
10. **Adiós, mis amigos.**

Answers on page 236.

LESSON 72

NEW WORD **agua**

MEANING *water*

The word **agua** is feminine in gender, but Spanish speakers use the masculine article **el** in front of it to make the pronunciation of this word sound clearer and easier to understand. So instead of **la agua**, you will see this: **el agua**.

EXERCISES:

1. **Yo quiero agua porque tengo sed.**
2. **Ellos quieren agua porque tienen sed.**
3. **Mi gato tiene hambre y quiere comida.**
4. **Buenas tardes, señor Smith.**
5. **Nosotros tenemos hambre, pero no tenemos dinero.**
6. **Yo tengo dos gatos.**
7. **El señor Jones tiene una hija y también tres hijos.**
8. **Los hombres tienen hambre, pero las mujeres no tienen hambre.**
9. **Mi hermana quiere el carro de mi papá.**
10. **Tú eres mi amiga.**

Answers on page 236.

LESSON 73

CONJUGATIONS

Not every Spanish verb has the same pattern of endings as the verbs you have studied so far. In Spanish, there are three main patterns of verb endings called *conjugations*. The first conjugation, second conjugation, and third conjugation each have certain rules we must remember when adding the appropriate endings. So far, the only action verbs you know (**yo tengo** and **yo quiero**) are from the second conjugation.

And when we learned about verb stems and personal endings, we learned that these are the personal endings for **yo tengo** and **yo quiero**:

	SINGULAR	PLURAL
FIRST PERSON	**-o**	**-emos**
SECOND PERSON	**-es**	**-éis**
THIRD PERSON	**-e**	**-en**

Notice how each of the personal endings in that chart started with the letter *e* (except for the first person singular). That's the way it is with all verbs from the second conjugation.

But things are a little different for verbs of the first conjugation. With first conjugation verbs, the personal endings start with the letter *a*. So if we made a chart of the personal endings from the first conjugation, it would look like this:

	SINGULAR	PLURAL
FIRST PERSON	**-o**	**-amos**
SECOND PERSON	**-as**	**-áis**
THIRD PERSON	**-a**	**-an**

So you see, the personal endings for the first conjugation are the same as the personal endings for the second conjugation, except for the beginning vowel.

Now let's look at a real example of a first conjugation verb. Here are the different forms of the verb **yo hablo**, which means *I speak*.

	SINGULAR	PLURAL
FIRST PERSON	**hablo**	**hablamos**
SECOND PERSON	**hablas**	**habláis**
THIRD PERSON	**habla**	**hablan**

Now for a side-by-side comparison. Let's compare the first person plural form of **yo hablo**, a first conjugation verb, with the first person plural form of **yo tengo**, a second conjugation verb.

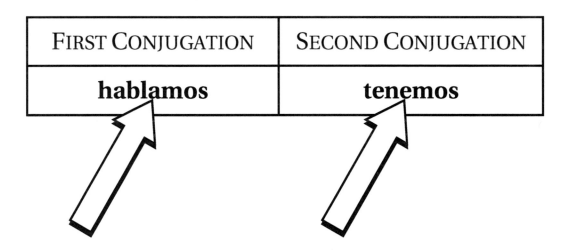

FIRST CONJUGATION	SECOND CONJUGATION
hablamos	**tenemos**

Again, we see that with **hablamos**, the personal ending starts with the letter *a*, but with **tenemos**, the personal ending starts with the letter *e*.

We still have a lot more to learn about conjugations, verb stems and personal endings. But for now, think about these personal endings, and we will learn more about how verbs work as we go through the rest of the book.

LESSON 74

NEW WORD **yo hablo**

MEANING *I speak*

PRONUNCIATION TIP: Remember that in Spanish, the letter *h* is always silent. So **hablo** will sound similar to *AHB-lo.*

In the last lesson, we learned about conjugations, and we saw that the personal endings for the first conjugation are a bit different than the personal endings of the second conjugation. Furthermore, we learned our first verb from the first conjugation, the verb **yo hablo**.

In this lesson, let's try to memorize the different forms of **yo hablo**, and get some practice using them in actual sentences.

This chart will help you familiarize yourself with the different forms of **yo hablo**.

	SINGULAR	PLURAL
FIRST PERSON	**yo hablo**	**nosotros/nosotras hablamos**
SECOND PERSON	**tú hablas**	**vosotros/vosotras habláis** (Spain only)
THIRD PERSON	**él/ella habla**	**ellos/ellas hablan**

In order to translate the exercises for this lesson, there are two important words you will need to know: First, **inglés**, which is the Spanish word for *English*. Also, **español**, which is the Spanish word for *Spanish*. Notice that the Spanish words **inglés** and **español** are not capitalized.

EXERCISES:

1. **Yo hablo inglés.**
2. **Tú hablas español.**
3. **Mis padres hablan inglés.**
4. **Nosotras hablamos español y también inglés.**
5. **El perro tiene hambre.**
6. **Ella quiere comida y agua.**
7. **Los niños tienen hambre y sed.**
8. **El gato de la mujer tiene hambre.**
9. **Ella no habla español.**
10. **Nosotros tenemos sed porque no tenemos agua.**

Answers on page 237.

LESSON 75

NEW WORD   **siempre**

MEANING   *always*

Siempre is your first Spanish adverb. An adverb is a word that describes how the action in a sentence is taking place.

EXERCISES:

1. **Yo siempre hablo español.**
2. **Mis hijos siempre quieren mi carro y mi dinero.**
3. **Ellos siempre quieren mi carro.**
4. **Tú siempre tienes hambre.**
5. **Mis amigos siempre hablan español.**
6. **Yo tengo hambre porque no tengo comida.**
7. **Nosotros no siempre hablamos inglés.**
8. **Ella tiene siete gatos.**
9. **Ellas no quieren un perro.**
10. **Tus niños quieren agua.**

Answers on page 237.

LESSON 76

NEW IDIOM   **todos los días**

MEANING   *every day*

Now let's learn how to say *every day* in Spanish:

Todos los días.

Todo is an adjective that means *all*. **Todos** is the masculine plural form of **todo**. The word **día** means *day*. Just by looking at the word **día**, you might think to yourself, "Well, it ends with the letter *a*, so it must be feminine. " However, the Spanish word **día** is masculine even though it looks feminine. There are exceptions to every rule, you know. And since **días** is masculine and plural, it needs to have **los** as its article.

If you translated **todos los días** word for word, it would say *all the days*. But idiomatically, it means *every day*.

Remember to do your Spanish homework **todos los días.**

EXERCISES:

1. **Yo hablo inglés todos los días.**
2. **Mi gato quiere mi comida todos los días.**
3. **Todos los días tú hablas español.**
4. **Ella tiene un perro y cuatro gatos.**
5. **Nosotros tenemos diez dólares.**
6. **Nosotros queremos agua porque tenemos sed.**
7. **Mi perro siempre quiere comida.**
8. **Ellas hablan español todos los días, pero nosotras hablamos inglés.**
9. **Los amigos de mi papá tienen hambre.**
10. **Tú eres mi hermana pero también eres mi amiga.**

Answers on page 237.

LESSON 77

NEW WORDS **yo compro**

MEANING *I buy*

Yo compro is a verb from the first conjugation, so it will have the following personal endings:

	SINGULAR	PLURAL
FIRST PERSON	**-o**	**-amos**
SECOND PERSON	**-as**	**-áis**
THIRD PERSON	**-a**	**-an**

Yo compro is an easy verb to learn, because the stem is the same for all six forms. It is not a stem-changing verb like **yo tengo**.

Using your knowledge of verb stems and personal endings, see if you can fill in the blanks below with the correct forms of **yo compro**. You may refer to the personal ending chart above if needed. A completed chart is on the next page so you can check your work when you finish.

Remember: the stem will always be **compr-** for this verb.

	SINGULAR	PLURAL
FIRST PERSON	**yo** _____	**nosotros/nosotras** _____
SECOND PERSON	**tú** _____	**vosotros/vosotras** _____
THIRD PERSON	**él/ella** _____	**ellos/ellas** _____

89

Hey! No peeking! Unless you are finished, of course.

Here is a completed chart with all the forms of **yo compro**.

	SINGULAR	PLURAL
FIRST PERSON	**yo compro**	**nosotros/nosotras compramos**
SECOND PERSON	**tú compras**	**vosotros/vosotras compráis** (Spain only)
THIRD PERSON	**él/ella compra**	**ellos/ellas compran**

Now that you are somewhat familiar with the different forms of **yo compro**, try these exercises.

EXERCISES:

1. **Todos los días yo compro comida.**
2. **Nosotros compramos comida todos los días.**
3. **Las mujeres compran comida todos los días.**
4. **El gato de mi hermana tiene hambre.**
5. **Yo no tengo comida y no tengo dinero.**
6. **Tú quieres agua porque tienes sed.**
7. **Nosotras hablamos español todos los días.**
8. **Mi hermana no habla inglés, pero habla español.**
9. **Buenos días, niños.**
10. **Tú siempre hablas inglés, pero yo siempre hablo español.**

Answers on page 238.

LESSON 78

ASKING QUESTIONS

Questions are an important part of any conversation. Fortunately for us, it is very easy to ask questions in Spanish. Imagine you have the following sentence:

Tú eres mi amigo.

In that sentence, which means *You are my friend*, the word **tú** is the subject and **eres** is the verb. To turn that sentence into a question, simply reverse the subject and the verb, like this:

¿Eres tú mi amigo?

Now it's a question, and it means *Are you my friend?* Notice that in written Spanish, a question will have a special upside-down question mark at the beginning of the sentence.

Here is another sentence to practice with:

Él tiene un gato.

In that sentence, which means *He has a cat,* **él** is the subject and **tiene** is the verb. So to make that sentence into a question, just reverse the subject and the verb, as we did before:

¿Tiene él un gato?

Now it's a question, and it means *Does he have a cat?*

You can do the same thing with any sentence, whether it has a pronoun or not, as in this example:

¿Tiene tu hermana un carro?

That question means *Does your sister have a car?* Notice how the subject and verb are reversed.

EXERCISES:

1. **Tú tienes un perro.**
2. **¿Tienes tú un perro?**
3. **Ellos compran comida todos los días.**
4. **¿Compran ellos comida todos los días?**
5. **Nosotros tenemos seis gatos.**
6. **¿Tenemos nosotros seis gatos?**
7. **Él habla español.**
8. **¿Habla él español?**
9. **Yo quiero el carro de mi papá.**
10. **Mi hija no tiene su carro.**

Answers on page 238.

LESSON 79

MEANING   *yes / no*

Now that you know how to ask questions, you need to know how to answer them. So read the following instructions very carefully:

Sí means *yes.* **No** means *no.*

We know this is a difficult lesson, but try not to get discouraged.

EXERCISES:

1. **¿Compras tú comida todos los días?**
2. **No, yo no compro comida todos los días.**
3. **¿Tiene tu hermano un niño?**
4. **Sí, mi hermano tiene tres hijos y también una hija.**
5. **¿Tienen hambre los hombres?**
6. **Sí, los hombres siempre tienen hambre.**
7. **¿Eres tú una madre?**
8. **No, yo no soy una madre porque no tengo niños.**
9. **¿Hablas tú español?**
10. **No, yo hablo inglés, pero mis hermanas hablan español todos los días.**

Answers on page 238.

LESSON 80

NEW WORDS **yo como**

MEANING *I eat*

Yo como is a regular verb of the second conjugation. The stem is always **com-**. Can you remember what the personal endings are for verbs of the second conjugation?

Learn the forms of **yo como** with this handy chart:

	SINGULAR	PLURAL
FIRST PERSON	**yo como**	**nosotros/nosotras comemos**
SECOND PERSON	**tú comes**	**vosotros/vosotras coméis** (Spain only)
THIRD PERSON	**él/ella come**	**ellos/ellas comen**

EXERCISES:

1. **Yo como comida todos los días.**
2. **Los muchachos comen comida todos los días.**
3. **Nosotros comemos todos los días.**
4. **¿Tiene hambre la señorita Smith?**
5. **No, la señorita Smith no tiene hambre, pero yo tengo hambre.**
6. **Ellos compran comida todos los días.**
7. **Los niños de mi hermana tienen cinco perros.**
8. **Buenas tardes, niños.**
9. **Yo tengo nueve hijos.**
10. **Nosotras siempre hablamos español.**

Answers on page 239.

LESSON 81

NEW WORDS **yo bebo**

MEANING *I drink*

Yo bebo is another verb of the second conjugation.

Learn the forms of **yo bebo** with this handy chart:

	SINGULAR	PLURAL
FIRST PERSON	**yo bebo**	**nosotros/nosotras bebemos**
SECOND PERSON	**tú bebes**	**vosotros/vosotras bebéis** (Spain only)
THIRD PERSON	**él/ella bebe**	**ellos/ellas beben**

EXERCISES:

1. **Todos los días yo bebo agua.**
2. **Ella tiene sed pero no quiere agua.**
3. **Mis hermanos hablan español todos los días.**
4. **¿Bebes tú agua todos los días?**
5. **Sí, bebo agua todos los días.**
6. **Mi papá tiene un perro y también dos gatos.**
7. **Nosotros comemos comida y bebemos agua todos los días.**
8. **Él come comida porque tiene hambre.**
9. **Mis padres compran comida todos los días.**
10. **Ellas son mis amigas.**

Answers on page 239.

LESSON 82

NEW IDIOM **todas las semanas**

MEANING *every week*

You already know how to say *every day*. Now, we are going to learn how to say *every week*. This is how it's done:

Todas las semanas.

Semana is a feminine word that means *week*. Since **semanas** is feminine and plural, it needs the article **las** and the adjective **todas**.

If you translated **todas las semanas** word for word, it would say *all the weeks*. But idiomatically, it means *every week*.

EXERCISES:

1. **Nosotros compramos comida todas las semanas.**
2. **Todas las semanas ellos compran comida.**
3. **Tus padres compran comida todas las semanas.**
4. **El perro de mi madre siempre tiene hambre.**
5. **Nosotros queremos comida y dinero.**
6. **Mis gatos quieren mi comida todos los días.**
7. **La muchacha habla inglés y español también.**
8. **Los hombres son mis hermanos.**
9. **¿Quiere tu hijo un carro?**
10. **Sí, mi hijo siempre quiere el carro de su padre.**

Answers on page 239.

LESSON 83

NEW WORDS   **yo trabajo**

MEANING   *I work*

Learn the different forms of **yo trabajo** with this handy chart:

	SINGULAR	PLURAL
FIRST PERSON	**yo trabajo**	**nosotros/nosotras trabajamos**
SECOND PERSON	**tú trabajas**	**vosotros/vosotras trabajáis** (Spain only)
THIRD PERSON	**él/ella trabaja**	**ellos/ellas trabajan**

EXERCISES:

1. **Yo trabajo todos los días.**
2. **Mis hermanas trabajan todos los días.**
3. **Nosotras compramos comida todas las semanas.**
4. **¿Trabajas tú todos los días?**
5. **Sí, yo trabajo todos los días.**
6. **Ellas son mis hermanas.**
7. **Ellos no hablan inglés, pero hablan español.**
8. **Nosotros tenemos sed porque no tenemos agua.**
9. **Mis hijos siempre tienen dinero porque trabajan todos los días.**
10. **Mis perros comen comida todos los días, y siempre beben agua.**

Answers on page 240.

LESSON 84

NEW WORD   **con**

MEANING   *with*

EXERCISES:

1. **Yo como con mis hermanas todas las semanas.**
2. **Él trabaja con mi hermano todos los días.**
3. **Yo hablo inglés con mis amigos, pero hablo español con mis padres.**
4. **Yo bebo agua todos los días.**
5. **Nosotros hablamos español todos los días.**
6. **Mis niños no hablan inglés, pero hablan español.**
7. **Yo tengo unas amigas.**
8. **Mis amigos tienen hambre y sed.**
9. **¿Tenemos nosotros comida?**
10. **No, nosotros no tenemos comida, pero tenemos agua.**

Answers on page 240.

LESSON 85

MORE ABOUT CON

In the last lesson, you got some experience using the word **con**. But there are two additional forms of **con** that we need to learn.

In Spanish, when you say *with me*, you don't say **con mi**. Instead, you use this special word: **conmigo**. Let's use **conmigo** in a sentence.

Él come conmigo todos los días (*He eats with me every day*).

Also, when you say *with you*, you don't say **con tú**. Instead, you use this special word: **contigo**. Let's use **contigo** in a sentence.

Yo como contigo todos los días (*I eat with you every day*).

Get some practice using **conmigo** and **contigo** by translating the exercises for this lesson.

EXERCISES:

1. **Ella come conmigo todas las semanas.**
2. **Ellos comen contigo todas las semanas.**
3. **¿Comen ellos contigo todos los días?**
4. **Sí, ellos comen conmigo todos los días.**
5. **Las muchachas quieren agua porque tienen sed.**
6. **Tu perro quiere agua.**
7. **Mi hermano trabaja conmigo todos los días.**
8. **Mi hermano habla español, pero yo hablo inglés.**
9. **El señor Smith trabaja todos los días.**
10. **Mis perros siempre beben agua.**

Answers on page 240.

LESSON 86

NEW WORDS   **yo voy**

MEANING   *I go*

Memorize all the forms of **yo voy** with this handy chart:

	SINGULAR	PLURAL
FIRST PERSON	**yo voy**	**nosotros/nosotras vamos**
SECOND PERSON	**tú vas**	**vosotros/vosotras vais** (Spain only)
THIRD PERSON	**él/ella va**	**ellos/ellas van**

EXERCISES:

1. **Yo voy contigo todas las semanas.**
2. **Tú vas conmigo todos los días.**
3. **Nosotros vamos todas las semanas, pero ellos van todos los días.**
4. **¿Vas tú todas las semanas?**
5. **Ellos van conmigo todos los días.**
6. **Él va con mis amigos todas las semanas.**
7. **¿Trabajan los hombres todos los días?**
8. **Sí, los hombres trabajan todos los días.**
9. **Nosotras bebemos agua todos los días.**
10. **Buenos días, señora Williams.**

Answers on page 241.

LESSON 87

NEW WORD **a**

MEANING *to*

Our new word for this lesson, **a**, is a very useful preposition that will really have you going places! But right now, we don't have any places to go, so let's learn a couple of new words.

The most common word for *store* in Spanish is **tienda**, and **banco** means *bank*.

Now let's use the word **a** in a couple of short examples:

> **a la tienda** *(to the store)*

In that example, we saw the preposition **a** followed by the article **la** since the word **tienda** is feminine. But when **a** is followed by a masculine noun, something special happens, as seen in this example:

> **a el banco** *(to the bank)*

In a sentence like that, when **a** is followed by the article **el**, you would take **a** and **el** and smash them together into the word **al**, like this:

> **al banco** *(to the bank)*

So while you translate the exercises for this lesson, remember that **a + el = al.**

EXERCISES:

1. **Yo voy a la tienda todas las semanas.**
2. **Mi madre va al banco todas las semanas.**
3. **¿Van tus padres a la tienda todos los días?**
4. **No, ellos van a la tienda todas las semanas.**
5. **Ella va al banco todas las semanas.**
6. **Yo voy a la tienda de mi padre todos los días.**
7. **Ella come conmigo todos los días.**
8. **Tú vas a la tienda conmigo todas las semanas.**

9. **Los muchachos y las muchachas trabajan todos los días.**
10. **Mis perros siempre tienen hambre.**

Answers on page 241.

LESSON 88

MEANING *I see*

Yo veo, our new word for this lesson, is from the second conjugation. Memorize all the forms of **yo veo** with this handy chart, then try the exercises.

	SINGULAR	PLURAL
FIRST PERSON	**yo veo**	**nosotros/nosotras vemos**
SECOND PERSON	**tú ves**	**vosotros/vosotras veis** (Spain only)
THIRD PERSON	**él/ella ve**	**ellos/ellas ven**

EXERCISES:

1. **Yo veo el carro.**
2. **Nosotros vemos tu perro todos los días.**
3. **¿Ves tú el dinero?**
4. **No, yo no veo el dinero.**
5. **Nosotros vamos a la tienda todas las semanas.**
6. **Tú trabajas con mi padre todos los días.**
7. **Ella bebe agua todos los días.**
8. **Buenas tardes, señorita Jones.**
9. **Mi hermana come conmigo todos los días.**
10. **Ellos siempre hablan español.**

Answers on page 241.

LESSON 89

MORE ABOUT A

A couple of lessons ago, we learned about the preposition **a**. We learned that **a** means *to*, and we used it in sentences to show where we were going. But in this lesson we need to learn another way to use the preposition **a**.

In a Spanish sentence, when the direct object is a human being, it is customary to put the preposition **a** in front of it, as demonstrated in the following example:

> **Yo veo a mi madre** *(I see my mother)*.

In this type of sentence, the word **a** does not translate to anything (in other words, it does not add anything to the English translation). This particular usage of the preposition **a** is called the *personal a* because it is only used when the direct object is a human being.

There are exceptions to this rule. For instance, with certain verbs, you do not follow this rule. One of those verbs is a verb you already know: **yo tengo**. Please examine the following example:

> **Yo tengo un amigo** *(I have a friend)*.

In that sentence, the direct object was a person, but it was the direct object of the verb **yo tengo**, so the personal **a** was not necessary.

Try these exercises, and if you get stuck, check the answer key.

EXERCISES:

1. **Yo veo a mis amigos todos los días.**
2. **¿Ves tú a tus amigos todos los días?**
3. **Ella ve a su padre todas las semanas.**
4. **Nosotros vemos a los niños todos los días.**
5. **Mi hijo compra comida todas las semanas.**
6. **¿Quieres tú un perro?**
7. **Sí, yo quiero un perro y también un gato.**
8. **Tú vas al banco con tu padre todas las semanas.**

9. **Mi perro no trabaja, pero siempre come.**
10. **Mis hijos quieren un gato.**

Answers on page 242.

LESSON 90

ASKING QUESTIONS WITHOUT PRONOUNS

You already know that Spanish speakers sometimes leave out pronouns when they make statements. When it is very clear and obvious whom the speaker is referring to, the pronoun is unnecessary and the speaker can leave it out if desired. And in this lesson, we will see that the same thing happens in questions.

So far, you have formed questions by reversing the subject and the verb, as seen in the following example:

¿Tienes tú un gato? *(Do you have a cat?)*

But when Spanish speakers ask questions, they don't always include the pronoun in the question. So they might ask that same question like this:

¿Tienes un gato? *(Do you have a cat?)*

Notice how in that example, the speaker left out the pronoun, which in this case was the word **tú**. So from now on, you will need to keep your eyes peeled for questions that do not have the pronoun.

EXERCISES:

1. **¿Tienes tú un carro?**
2. **¿Tienes un carro?**
3. **¿Tenemos nosotros cuatro perros?**
4. **¿Tenemos cuatro perros?**
5. **¿Ves tú al señor Smith todos los días?**
6. **¿Ves al señor Smith todos los días?**
7. **¿Vas tú a la tienda todas las semanas?**
8. **¿Vas a la tienda todas las semanas?**
9. **Yo voy a la tienda contigo todas las semanas.**
10. **Mi hermana quiere el carro de mis padres.**

Answers on page 242.

LESSON 91

NEW WORDS **centro comercial**

MEANING *mall, shopping center*

PRONUNCIATION TIP: In the word **comercial**, the accent falls on the last syllable.

Centro comercial is masculine. In this book, we will translate **centro comercial** as *mall.*

EXERCISES:

1. **Nosotras vamos al centro comercial todas las semanas.**
2. **Yo voy al centro comercial con mis amigos todos los días.**
3. **Mis hijas van al centro comercial todos los días.**
4. **¿Vas al banco todas las semanas?**
5. **Sí, voy al banco todas las semanas.**
6. **Ellos ven a mi papá todos los días.**
7. **Mis hijos quieren un gato.**
8. **Tú vas conmigo al centro comercial todas las semanas porque somos amigos.**
9. **¿Habla tu madre español?**
10. **No, mi madre no habla español.**

Answers on page 242.

LESSON 92

NEW IDIOM **a menudo**

MEANING *often*

This expression, which consists of two words, is another adverb just like **siempre**.

EXERCISES:

1. **Yo voy al banco a menudo.**
2. **Tú no vas a la tienda a menudo, pero yo voy a la tienda todas las semanas.**
3. **¿Hablas inglés a menudo?**
4. **Sí, yo siempre hablo inglés, pero mis amigos hablan español.**
5. **¿Ves a tus hermanas a menudo?**
6. **Sí, yo veo a mis hermanas todas las semanas.**
7. **Nosotros bebemos agua a menudo porque siempre tenemos sed.**
8. **Nosotros vemos a los hijos de mi hermano todas las semanas.**
9. **Yo voy contigo al centro comercial todas las semanas.**
10. **Las mujeres trabajan todos los días.**

Answers on page 243.

LESSON 93

NEW WORD **nunca**

MEANING *never*

Nunca is another adverb just like **siempre** and **a menudo**.

EXERCISES:

1. Yo nunca voy al centro comercial, pero mis padres van todas las semanas.
2. ¿Vas a la tienda a menudo?
3. No, nunca voy a la tienda.
4. Nosotros vamos al centro comercial a menudo, pero nunca tenemos dinero.
5. ¿Compras comida a menudo?
6. Sí, yo voy a la tienda todos los días.
7. Mi perro bebe agua a menudo porque tiene sed.
8. Los amigos de mi padre trabajan todos los días.
9. Yo no quiero un perro, porque los perros siempre tienen hambre.
10. Yo veo a mis amigos todos los días.

Answers on page 243.

LESSON 94

NEW WORD **sin**

MEANING *without*

PRONUNCIATION TIP: The word **sin** sounds like the English word *seen*.

Sin is another preposition just like **con.**

EXERCISES:

1. **Yo nunca voy al centro comercial sin dinero.**
2. **Mi mamá nunca va al banco sin dinero.**
3. **Yo nunca voy al centro comercial sin mis amigos.**
4. **Las mujeres hablan español todos los días.**
5. **¿Va él al centro comercial a menudo?**
6. **Sí, él va al centro comercial todas las semanas.**
7. **Mi hermano y sus amigos siempre van al centro comercial.**
8. **La hermana de mi padre nunca va a la tienda sin dinero.**
9. **Nosotros vamos al centro comercial con mis padres todas las semanas.**
10. **Yo veo a mis amigos todos los días.**

Answers on page 243.

LESSON 95

NEW WORD **parque**

MEANING *park*

PRONUNCIATION TIP: **Parque** has two syllables. The accent is on the first syllable, so it sounds like *PAR-keh*.

Parque, our new word for this lesson, is masculine.

EXERCISES:

1. **Yo nunca voy al parque.**
2. **Ellas van al parque todas las semanas.**
3. **¿Vas tú al parque con tus amigos a menudo?**
4. **Sí, yo siempre voy al parque con mis amigos.**
5. **Tú eres mi amiga.**
6. **Nosotros siempre hablamos español, pero mis padres nunca hablan español.**
7. **¿Vas a la tienda a menudo?**
8. **Sí, voy a la tienda contigo todas las semanas.**
9. **Nosotras nunca vamos al centro comercial sin dinero.**
10. **El perro de mi papá siempre tiene hambre.**

Answers on page 244.

LESSON 96

NEW WORD **playa**

MEANING *beach*

Playa, our new word for this lesson, is feminine.

EXERCISES:

1. **Mis amigos van a la playa a menudo.**
2. **¿Vas a la playa a menudo?**
3. **No, yo nunca voy a la playa.**
4. **Él va a la playa con sus padres todas las semanas.**
5. **Ellos siempre van a la playa, pero nosotros siempre vamos al parque.**
6. **Tú nunca vas al centro comercial sin dinero.**
7. **Nosotros somos amigos.**
8. **Yo quiero el carro de mi hermana.**
9. **Ellos ven a la señora Jones todas las semanas.**
10. **Él nunca va a la tienda contigo.**

Answers on page 244.

LESSON 97

FORMAL AND INFORMAL SPEECH

If you met the queen of England, would you speak to her the same way as you would speak to your friends? Probably not!

With your friends, you would probably speak informally—perhaps using slang words or other types of speech that close friends or family typically use with one another. However, if you met someone important, or a stranger, you would probably speak in a more formal way. In the Spanish language, there is certain way to speak to others that is considered more formal than the usual way of speaking. To help explain this more formal way of speaking, let's use our imagination a little.

Imagine for a moment that you are in a palace in England. The queen's butler is in the kitchen, taking a break. The cook, who is also taking a break, sits nearby sipping a cup of coffee. The butler says to his friend the cook, "You usually drink tea."

Later that same day, the queen asks for some coffee. The butler says to the queen, "Your Majesty usually drinks tea."

Go back and reread each of the butler's statements, paying special attention to the subject and the verb of each sentence. What differences do you notice?

Many lessons ago, we learned about a certain quality that verbs have called *person*. First person, second person, and third person are three different aspects or relationships with the speaker that a given verb can have. When the butler asked the cook if he wanted another cup of tea, the butler spoke to him as you would expect—in the second person, like this:

<u>You</u> usually <u>drink</u> tea.

Since the butler was the cook's friend, he spoke to him in a way that people would ordinarily speak to one another—using the word *you* along with the second person verb *drink*. But do you think it would be acceptable for the butler to speak to the queen in the same way that he would address a friend or fellow worker? No. Instead, our imaginary butler spoke to the queen like this:

<u>Your Majesty</u> usually <u>drinks</u> tea.

113

In this example, the butler addressed the queen in a formal way—using the special title *Your Majesty*, along with the third person verb *drinks*. If the butler had addressed the queen in the same way as he addressed the cook, with the word *you*, it might have sounded out of place—too informal to show the proper level of respect that is appropriate for a queen.

So, what can we learn from our imaginary butler? And how does it relate to learning Spanish? Well, here it is: *To speak to someone in a very formal way, address that person with a special title of respect, along with a third person verb.*

In each of the following exercises, a formal style of speech is being used. You must choose the correct verb to agree with the special titles being used.

EXERCISES:

1. Your Majesty [have / has] a cup of tea already.
2. Your Honor [are / is] welcome to see the document.
3. Your Excellency [go / goes] to meetings every day.
4. [Have / Has] Your Honor heard enough testimony?
5. Your Majesty usually [prefer / prefers] Earl Grey tea.

Answers on page 244.

LESSON 98

NEW WORD   **usted**

MEANING   *you* (formal, singular)

In the last lesson, we learned that we usually speak to others in the second person. But to speak to someone in a very formal way, we address that person with a special title of respect followed by a third person verb.

In Spanish, if you want to address a friend, family member or someone else you know, you would say **tú**. But if you want to address someone you don't know very well, or someone important, you would instead use the special title of respect **usted**.

The word **usted** is hundreds of years old. At first it was **vuestra merced**, which means *Your Mercy*. As time passed, **vuestra merced** changed little by little into **usted**. Today, **usted** just means *you*, but it's used to show respect to the person being addressed.

When you address someone as **usted**, you must use a third person verb. So, you would not say **usted eres** because that would be incorrect—after all, you would never say *Your Mercy are*. Instead, you would say *Your Mercy is*. Likewise, when you use **usted**, use it with a third person verb, like this:

>   **Usted es** *(you are).*

Notice how in that example, the word **usted** was accompanied by the third person verb **es**, not the second person verb **eres**.

We have provided a chart on the next page to help you understand how **usted** fits in with the other verbs you know. Notice that even though **usted es** is third person, we use it to address people as though it were second person.

	SINGULAR	PLURAL
FIRST PERSON	**yo soy**	**nosotros/nosotras somos**
SECOND PERSON	**tú eres**	**vosotros/vosotras sois** (Spain only)
THIRD PERSON	**él/ella es** **usted es**	**ellos/ellas son**

So whenever you want to speak to someone in a formal way, use **usted** plus a third person verb, as in the following examples.

> **Usted es** *(You are).*
> **Usted tiene un carro** *(You have a car).*
> **¿Va usted al centro comercial todas las semanas?** *(Do you go to the mall every week?)*

In the exercises for this lesson, let's get some practice speaking in this formal manner using **usted** with third person verbs.

EXERCISES:

1. **Usted es.**
2. **Usted es el señor Johnson.**
3. **¿Es usted el señor Johnson?**
4. **Usted tiene un gato.**
5. **¿Tiene usted un gato?**
6. **Usted habla inglés.**
7. **¿Habla usted español?**
8. **¿Va usted a la playa a menudo?**
9. **Usted nunca va al banco.**
10. **¿Tiene usted unos niños?**

Answers on page 245.

LESSON 99

NEW WORD **ustedes**

MEANING *y'all*

In the last lesson we learned that **usted** is used to speak to someone in a formal way. Now in this lesson, we are going to learn the plural form of **usted**, which is **ustedes**.

Before we go any further, we need to discuss a small difference in the way Spanish is spoken in different places. In Spain, **ustedes** is (as you would expect) a formal way to address multiple people. However in the Americas, the word **ustedes** has gradually lost its sense of formality. In fact, **ustedes** is now the only way to address multiple people in every situation, whether formal or informal.

Think waaaaaaaaaaay back to lesson 36. In that lesson, we told you that the pronouns **vosotros** and **vosotras** were used only in Spain, and that in the Americas they have a different way of addressing multiple people that we would tell you about later. Well, **ustedes** is the way we were talking about! Now that you know the word **ustedes**, you know how to address multiple people the way they do it in the Americas.

So here is the bottom line: If you are in Spain, and you want to address multiple people, you would say **vosotros** or **vosotras** in an informal situation or **ustedes** if you wanted to be formal. But in the Americas, you would use **ustedes** regardless of the situation.

Keep in mind that **ustedes**, like **usted**, is a third person word and must be accompanied by a third person verb.

On the next page, we have provided a chart to help you see how **ustedes** fits in with the verbs you already know.

	SINGULAR	PLURAL
FIRST PERSON	yo soy	nosotros/nosotras somos
SECOND PERSON	tú eres	vosotros/vosotras sois (Spain only)
THIRD PERSON	él/ella es usted es	ellos/ellas son ustedes son

In these exercises, let's get some practice working with **ustedes**.

EXERCISES:

1. **Ustedes son mis amigos.**
2. **¿Tienen ustedes un gato?**
3. **Ustedes van a la playa todas las semanas.**
4. **¿Van ustedes al centro comercial a menudo?**
5. **Ustedes nunca van al centro comercial sin dinero.**
6. **¿Es usted el señor Smith?**
7. **¿Hablan ustedes inglés?**
8. **Nosotros nunca vamos al parque sin comida y sin agua.**
9. **Mis padres van al centro comercial conmigo a menudo.**
10. **Yo hablo español contigo, pero hablo inglés con mis padres.**

Answers on page 245.

LESSON 100

NEW WORD   **trabajo**

MEANING   *work, job*

We already have used **yo trabajo** as a verb, but the word **trabajo** is also a noun. **Trabajo** is masculine, and it can mean either *work* or *job* depending on the context.

EXERCISES:

1. **Yo voy a mi trabajo todos los días.**
2. **Yo quiero un trabajo.**
3. **Mi padre va a su trabajo todos los días.**
4. **Mi amigo quiere un trabajo porque él quiere un carro.**
5. **Yo trabajo todos los días.**
6. **La señora Jones nunca va al centro comercial sin su dinero.**
7. **¿Van ustedes al parque todas las semanas?**
8. **No, nosotros nunca vamos al parque, pero vamos a la playa a menudo.**
9. **Mi hermana tiene unos perros y también un gato.**
10. **¿Es usted la señorita Smith?**

Answers on page 245.

LESSON 101

NEW WORD **familia**

MEANING *family*

Familia is a feminine noun.

EXERCISES:

1. Tu familia va a la tienda todas las semanas.
2. Mi hermano va a la playa con su familia todas las semanas.
3. Mi familia come conmigo todos los días.
4. La mujer y los niños son mi familia.
5. Yo tengo un trabajo y un carro.
6. Usted es el señor Williams.
7. Ustedes son mis amigos.
8. ¿Es usted la señora Jones?
9. ¿Va usted al parque todas las semanas?
10. Ella va a su trabajo todos los días.

Answers on page 246.

LESSON 102

MORE ABOUT SU

When we studied formal speech, we learned how to use third person verbs to address someone. Although speaking directly to someone would ordinarily involve the use of second person verbs, we use third person verbs with the special title **usted**.

Well, with the word **su**, the situation is somewhat similar. In informal speech, we use the word **su** to mean *his, her* or *its*. But in formal speech, **su** means *your*. Even though **su** is a third person word, in formal speech we use it as though it were a second person word.

Let's study the following example:

> **Usted va a la tienda con su familia todas las semanas** *(You go to the store with your family every week).*

In this example, the speaker is addressing someone in a formal way, using **usted** plus a third person verb. So to say the word *your*, the speaker would not say **tu**, but instead he would continue speaking in the third person, using the word **su**, which would mean **your**. In this context, we know that the word **su** means *your* because the speaker is using the word **su** in the context of formal speech which makes use of third person forms.

If we took that same example sentence and rewrote it using informal speech, it would read like this:

> **Tú vas a la tienda con tu familia todas las semanas** *(You go to the store with your family every week).*

So here is the bottom line: **tu** is the informal way to say *your*, and **su** is the formal way to say *your*.

As you translate each of the following exercises, use the context to decide if **su** means *his* or *her*, or if the word **su** is being used to mean *your* in the context of formal speech.

EXERCISES:

1. ¿Va usted a la playa con su hermana todas las semanas?
2. El hombre va a su trabajo todos los días.
3. Usted va al banco con sus hijos todas las semanas.
4. ¿Va usted al centro comercial con sus amigos todas las semanas?
5. Nosotros bebemos agua todos los días.
6. ¿Tiene usted su perro?
7. ¿Va usted al parque con su familia a menudo?
8. ¿Hablan ustedes español?
9. ¿Habla usted español con sus amigos?
10. Yo quiero agua porque tengo sed.

Answers on page 246.

LESSON 103

NEW WORD **yo camino**

MEANING *I walk*

Study the different forms of **yo camino** with this chart:

	SINGULAR	PLURAL
FIRST PERSON	**yo camino**	**nosotros/nosotras caminamos**
SECOND PERSON	**tú caminas**	**vosotros/vosotras camináis** (Spain only)
THIRD PERSON	**él/ella camina** **usted camina** (used as 2nd person)	**ellos/ellas caminan** **ustedes caminan** (used as 2nd person)

EXERCISES:

1. **Mi familia camina al parque todos los días.**
2. **¿Camina usted a la playa todas las semanas?**
3. **Mis amigos caminan a la playa todas las semanas.**
4. **Yo camino a la tienda con mi mamá todas las semanas.**
5. **Yo camino al parque con usted a menudo.**
6. **Ella nunca camina a la playa conmigo.**
7. **Nosotros caminamos a la playa a menudo, pero nunca vamos al parque.**
8. **Él camina a la playa con sus amigos todas las semanas.**
9. **¿Caminan ustedes al parque a menudo?**
10. **Yo no tengo un carro porque no tengo un trabajo.**

Answers on page 246.

LESSON 104

INFINITIVES

An infinitive is the word *to* plus a verb. Here are some examples of infinitives:

> to walk
> to eat
> to run
> to be

Let's examine some of the different ways infinitives are used:

> I like <u>to sing</u>.
> I want <u>to be</u> a teacher.
> <u>To eat</u> a watermelon is sheer delight.
> I am unable <u>to finish</u> my homework.
> I want <u>to play</u> checkers.

Try to locate the infinitive in each of the exercises below. But be careful! A few of the exercises do not have infinitives. Can you tell which ones they are?

EXERCISES:

1. I do not like to wash the dishes.
2. They want to play a different game.
3. I went to the store.
4. Charles wants to be a policeman.
5. To forgive is divine.
6. She wants to return that sweater to the store.
7. Jenny would like to play the clarinet.
8. We will not go to the party.
9. She will go to the furniture store to buy a chair.
10. Throw the ball to Jeremy.

Answers on page 247.

LESSON 105

NEW WORD   **comprar**

MEANING   *to buy*

In English, it takes two words to express an infinitive: the word *to* and a verb. In Spanish, however, it only takes one word to express an infinitive.

In this lesson, we learn our first Spanish infinitive: the word **comprar**. Examine the ending of the word **comprar**. Instead of ending in **–o** or some other personal ending, it ends in **-ar**. Let's use **comprar** in a sentence:

> **Yo quiero comprar comida** *(I want to buy food)*.

In the following exercises, get some practice working with the infinitive **comprar**, and in the next lesson we will learn some more infinitives.

EXERCISES:

1. **Yo quiero comprar un carro.**
2. **Ellos quieren comprar comida.**
3. **Nosotros no queremos comprar un gato.**
4. **Él va a la tienda todas las semanas porque quiere comprar comida.**
5. **Ella quiere comprar el carro de su hermano.**
6. **Mi familia nunca camina a la playa sin agua.**
7. **Señor, ¿es la señora Jones su hermana?**
8. **Ustedes son mis hermanos y hermanas.**
9. **Hola, señor—¿es usted el señor Smith?**
10. **Sí, yo soy el señor Smith.**

Answers on page 247.

L E S S O N 1 0 6

MORE ABOUT CONJUGATIONS AND INFINITIVES

A few lessons ago, we learned that there are three main groups of verbs called *conjugations.* The first conjugation, second conjugation and third conjugation each have certain characteristics. You can tell which conjugation a verb belongs to by looking at the infinitive form of the verb. For verbs that belong to the first conjugation, the infinitive ends in **–ar**. For verbs that belong to the second conjugation, the infinitive ends in **–er**. For verbs that belong to the third conjugation, the infinitive ends in **–ir.** Most of the verbs you have learned up to this point are from the first and second conjugations. You only know one third conjugation verb so far, and that's **yo voy**. In this book, we will focus mainly on the first and second conjugations. So for now, don't worry too much about the third conjugation.

Let's put the verbs you already know into a chart, organized by conjugation, so you can see which verbs belongs to each conjugation. After each verb, the infinitive form of that verb is shown in parenthesis. Please take a few minutes to familiarize yourself with this chart. **Comprar**, the infinitive you studied in the last lesson, belongs to the first conjugation.

FIRST CONJUGATION (Infinitive ends in **–ar**)	SECOND CONJUGATION (Infinitive ends in **–er**)	THIRD CONJUGATION (Infinitive ends in **–ir**)
yo compro (comprar) **yo hablo (hablar)** **yo trabajo (trabajar)** **yo camino (caminar)**	**yo soy (ser)** **yo tengo (tener)** **yo quiero (querer)** **yo como (comer)** **yo bebo (beber)** **yo veo (ver)**	**yo voy (ir)**

Give this some thought, and in the next lesson we will learn a bit more about infinitives and how we can use them.

L E S S O N   1 0 7

MORE ABOUT VERB STEMS

In the last lesson, we learned how to tell which conjugation an infinitive is from by determining if it ends in **–ar**, **–er** or **–ir**. But infinitives do much more than just tell us which conjugation a verb is from—infinitives can also help us find the stem of a verb.

Remember a while ago when we learned about verb stems? The stem is the first part of the verb, to which you add the personal endings. Well, the infinitive is what we use to find the stem of any given verb. To find the stem of any verb, just take the infinitive, and remove the final two letters, which will be either **–ar**, **–er** or **–ir**, depending on what conjugation the verb is from. After you have taken away these final two letters, the part that is left is the stem of the verb. It's just that easy!

For regular verbs, once you have the stem, it's easy to figure out all the other forms of the verb because all you have to do is add the personal endings for that conjugation. Just for review, here are the personal endings for the first conjugation:

	SINGULAR	PLURAL
FIRST PERSON	**-o**	**-amos**
SECOND PERSON	**-as**	**-áis**
THIRD PERSON	**-a**	**-an**

Just for practice, let's use the stem and the personal endings to produce the six different present tense forms of a verb from scratch. Let's start with a verb from the first conjugation…oh, let's say…**yo compro**.

First, take the infinitive form, which is **comprar**.

comprar

Then, remove the final two letters, which would be **–ar**.

compr-

Then, add the personal endings:

	SINGULAR	PLURAL
FIRST PERSON	**compr + o = compro**	**compr + amos = compramos**
SECOND PERSON	**compr + as = compras**	**compr + áis = compráis**
THIRD PERSON	**compr + a = compra**	**compr + an = compran**

Success! Now, let's try it with a verb from the second conjugation…like…**yo bebo**. But before we start, let's review the personal endings from the second conjugation:

	SINGULAR	PLURAL
FIRST PERSON	**-o**	**-emos**
SECOND PERSON	**-es**	**-éis**
THIRD PERSON	**-e**	**-en**

First, take the infinitive form, which is **beber**.

beber

Then, remove the final two letters, which would be **–er**.

beb-

Then, add the personal endings:

	SINGULAR	PLURAL
FIRST PERSON	beb + o = bebo	beb + emos = bebemos
SECOND PERSON	beb + es = bebes	beb + éis = bebéis
THIRD PERSON	beb + e = bebe	beb + en = beben

Hey! It worked again!

One last note: the verbs **yo tengo, yo quiero** and **yo voy** are irregular verbs (**yo quiero** is a stem-changing or shoe verb). When a verb is irregular, that means it does not fit the expected pattern. So this method will not work with those verbs. For irregular verbs, you must simply memorize their various forms by repetition.

Okay, so now you have seen two examples—now it's time to get out a pencil and some paper and try this yourself. This will help you to develop some major Spanish skills!

For each of these regular verbs, use the infinitive and the personal endings for the appropriate conjugation to create all six present tense forms of that verb.

EXERCISES:

1. **yo hablo/hablar**
2. **yo trabajo/trabajar**
3. **yo como/comer**
4. **yo camino/caminar**

Answers on page 247.

LESSON 108

NEW WORD **ropa**

MEANING *clothes*

The word **ropa** is singular, even though we translate it into English as the plural word *clothes*. And it's feminine, too.

In this lesson you will see lots of infinitives, so keep your eyes peeled! Remember that **ir** is the infinitive form of **yo voy**. So **ir** means *to go*.

EXERCISES:

1. **Yo quiero comprar ropa.**
2. **¿Papá, quieres comprar ropa?**
3. **Nosotros no queremos caminar a la tienda.**
4. **Nosotros queremos tener un gato.**
5. **¿Tienen ustedes hambre?**
6. **¿Tiene usted un trabajo?**
7. **La familia del señor Jones va a la playa a menudo.**
8. **Él quiere ir a la tienda.**
9. **Mi gato nunca trabaja, pero siempre tiene hambre.**
10. **Yo quiero beber agua porque tengo sed.**

Answers on page 248.

LESSON 109

NEW WORD **hoy**

MEANING *today*

PRONUNCIATION TIP: In Spanish the letter *h* is always silent.

EXERCISES:

1. **Yo quiero ir a la playa hoy.**
2. **Nosotros no queremos ir al banco hoy.**
3. **Tú quieres caminar a la playa todos los días.**
4. **Mis amigos quieren ir al centro comercial.**
5. **Ellas quieren comprar ropa.**
6. **¿Va usted al centro comercial con su familia a menudo?**
7. **No, nosotros nunca vamos al centro comercial.**
8. **Somos los niños de la señora Jones.**
9. **Ella nunca va al parque sin su perro.**
10. **Yo quiero tener un gato, pero no quiero un perro.**

Answers on page 248.

LESSON 110

NEW WORDS   **yo necesito / necesitar**

MEANING   *I need / to need*

The infinitive form, **necesitar**, ends in **-ar**, so that means that this verb is from the first conjugation.

Just for review, here are the personal endings for the first conjugation again:

	SINGULAR	PLURAL
FIRST PERSON	**-o**	**-amos**
SECOND PERSON	**-as**	**-áis**
THIRD PERSON	**-a**	**-an**

Using the knowledge you have gained, can you figure out all the forms of this verb?

EXERCISES:

1. **Yo necesito beber agua porque tengo sed.**
2. **Mi papá necesita comprar comida.**
3. **Ellos necesitan ir a la tienda porque necesitan comprar ropa.**
4. **Nosotros queremos ir a la playa hoy.**
5. **¿Tiene usted una familia, señor Williams?**
6. **Mis padres quieren tener un perro.**
7. **El perro de mis padres siempre tiene hambre.**
8. **La muchacha quiere ir al centro comercial con sus amigas.**
9. **¿Caminas tú a la playa a menudo?**
10. **Sí, yo voy a la playa todos los días.**

Answers on page 248.

LESSON 111

NEW WORD **mañana**

MEANING *tomorrow*

PRONUNCIATION TIP: The little mark over the letter *n* is called a *tilde*. In Spanish, whenever the letter *n* has a tilde, it will sound like the *n* in the word *canyon*. So **mañana** will sound similar to *man-YAH-na*.

EXERCISES:

1. **Yo necesito ir al banco mañana.**
2. **Nosotros queremos ir a la playa mañana.**
3. **Ella necesita ir a la tienda hoy, pero mañana ella quiere ir al banco.**
4. **Yo necesito ir al centro comercial porque quiero comprar ropa.**
5. **¿Caminan ustedes a la playa a menudo?**
6. **¿Quieren ustedes ir al parque?**
7. **¿Quieres ir al centro comercial conmigo?**
8. **No, yo nunca voy al centro comercial.**
9. **Nosotros queremos hablar español.**
10. **Tengo hambre.**

Answers on page 249.

L E S S O N   1 1 2

NEW WORDS **yo puedo / poder**

MEANING *I am able, I can / to be able*

In Spanish, we use the verb **yo puedo** to say that we are able to do something. But **yo puedo** cannot do anything by itself. It needs an infinitive to complete its meaning. Consider the following examples:

> **Yo puedo trabajar** *(I am able to work* OR *I can work).*
> **Yo puedo caminar** *(I am able to walk* OR *I can walk).*
> **Yo no puedo comprar ropa** *(I am not able to buy clothes* OR *I cannot buy clothes).*

In each of these examples, **yo puedo** worked with an infinitive to show what activity the subject of the sentence was or was not able to do.

EXERCISES:

1. **Yo puedo caminar al parque.**
2. **Yo puedo hablar español.**
3. **Yo puedo ir al parque mañana.**
4. **Yo no puedo comprar un carro.**
5. **Yo puedo trabajar.**
6. **Nosotros queremos comprar ropa hoy.**
7. **Ella no necesita comprar ropa, pero quiere ir al centro comercial.**
8. **Mis gatos son mis amigos.**
9. **¿Tiene usted unos niños?**
10. **Nunca vamos a la playa.**

Answers on page 249.

LESSON 113

THE OTHER FORMS OF YO PUEDO

Now it's time to learn the other forms of **yo puedo**, since **yo puedo** is only the first person singular form of the verb. The infinitive form of this verb is **poder**, which means *to be able*.

Here are all the forms of **yo puedo/poder** in a handy chart:

	SINGULAR	PLURAL
FIRST PERSON	**yo puedo**	**nosotros/nosotras podemos**
SECOND PERSON	**tú puedes**	**vosotros/vosotras podéis** (Spain only)
THIRD PERSON	**él/ella puede** **usted puede** (used as 2nd person)	**ellos/ellas pueden** **ustedes pueden** (used as 2nd person)

Using the infinitive form, **poder**, we can determine that the stem for this verb is **pod-**. But only the first person plural and second person plural are based on this stem, while the other forms are based on an altered stem, which is **pued-**. That's because, like **yo tengo/tener**, **yo puedo/poder** is a stem-changing verb, or shoe verb!

So that means it's time to draw a shoe! Draw a shoe around the forms of **yo puedo/poder** that have the changed stem.

puedo   **podemos**

puedes   **podéis**

puede   **pueden**

You're not done yet! Do these exercises! Then you're done (for now).

EXERCISES:

1. **Tú no puedes caminar al banco.**
2. **Ella puede comprar un carro.**
3. **Nosotros podemos ir al parque, pero no podemos ir a la playa.**
4. **¿Puedes tú ir conmigo a la tienda?**
5. **Ellos no pueden tener un gato.**
6. **Nosotros necesitamos un perro.**
7. **Yo no puedo ir al centro comercial mañana, pero puedo ir hoy.**
8. **¿Quieren ustedes ir al centro comercial?**
9. **Ustedes ven a la señora Jones todas las semanas.**
10. **Nosotros no vamos a la tienda sin dinero.**

Answers on page 249.

LESSON 114

NEW WORD **escuela**

MEANING *school*

Escuela, our new word for this lesson, is feminine.

EXERCISES:

1. **Nosotros caminamos a la escuela todos los días.**
2. **¡Yo no quiero ir a la escuela hoy!**
3. **Yo camino a la escuela con mis amigos todos los días.**
4. **Los muchachos no quieren trabajar hoy.**
5. **Mi perro quiere ir a la escuela conmigo.**
6. **¿Quieres tú caminar conmigo a la escuela?**
7. **Yo no quiero ir a la tienda hoy porque no necesito comida.**
8. **Tú no puedes ir a la tienda sin dinero.**
9. **¿Necesitan ustedes agua?**
10. **Ella quiere ir al centro comercial mañana porque quiere comprar ropa.**

Answers on page 250.

LESSON 115

NEW WORD **libro**

MEANING *book*

Libro, our new word for this lesson, is masculine.

EXERCISES:

1. **Tengo diez libros.**
2. **Yo quiero comprar unos libros.**
3. **Mis hermanas quieren comprar unos libros, pero no pueden porque no tienen dinero.**
4. **Mis perros caminan a la escuela conmigo todos los días.**
5. **Mi gato tiene hambre.**
6. **Yo necesito mis libros hoy porque necesito ir a la escuela.**
7. **Tú tienes el libro de mi hermana.**
8. **Nosotros no queremos ir a la escuela mañana.**
9. **Él quiere ver a sus amigos.**
10. **¿Va usted al parque a menudo?**

Answers on page 250.

LESSON 116

NEW WORDS **yo cargo / cargar**

MEANING   *I carry / to carry*

The infinitive form, **cargar**, ends in **-ar**, so that means it is from the first conjugation. Using your knowledge of infinitives, stems and personal endings, can you figure out all the forms of this new verb?

EXERCISES:

1. **Yo cargo mis libros a la escuela todos los días.**
2. **Nosotros siempre cargamos comida y agua al parque.**
3. **Mis padres siempre cargan dinero.**
4. **Yo camino con mis perros todos los días.**
5. **Él no puede cargar a mi hermano.**
6. **Nosotros necesitamos unos libros.**
7. **Ella no quiere caminar a la playa mañana.**
8. **¿Cargan ustedes comida y agua?**
9. **No, pero tenemos hambre y sed.**
10. **Yo quiero beber agua.**

Answers on page 250.

LESSON 117

NEW WORDS **yo leo / leer**

MEANING *I read / to read*

The infinitive form, **leer**, ends in **–er** so you know it's from the second conjugation.

And, **yo leo/leer** is a regular verb, so try to figure out all the forms on your own before you look at the chart.

	SINGULAR	PLURAL
FIRST PERSON	**yo leo**	**nosotros/nosotras leemos**
SECOND PERSON	**tú lees**	**vosotros/vosotras leéis** (Spain only)
THIRD PERSON	**él/ella lee** **usted lee** (used as 2nd person)	**ellos/ellas leen** **ustedes leen** (used as 2nd person)

EXERCISES:

1. **Yo leo un libro todas las semanas.**
2. **¿Quieres tú leer un libro?**
3. **Nosotros no queremos leer un libro hoy.**
4. **Mis niños quieren leer libros, pero no quieren trabajar.**
5. **Tú puedes leer el libro.**
6. **¿Quieren ustedes ir a la escuela?**
7. **Tú necesitas ir a la escuela mañana.**
8. **Nosotros cargamos libros todos los días.**
9. **¿Tiene usted el libro de mi hermano?**
10. **Ellas pueden leer.**

Answers on page 251.

LESSON 118

NEW WORD   **periódico**

MEANING   *newspaper*

The word **periódico** is masculine.

EXERCISES:

1. **Yo quiero leer el periódico.**
2. **Mis padres leen el periódico todos los días.**
3. **Yo tengo un trabajo; yo cargo los periódicos todos los días.**
4. **Mi madre lee el periódico con mi padre todos los días.**
5. **Mi hermano no puede leer el periódico.**
6. **Yo quiero el periódico de mi padre.**
7. **¿Va usted a la playa con su familia todas las semanas?**
8. **Sí, mi familia siempre va conmigo a la playa.**
9. **Ellos no pueden cargar los libros hoy.**
10. **Yo no quiero ir a la escuela mañana.**

Answers on page 251.

LESSON 119

NEW WORD **iglesia**

MEANING *church*

Iglesia is feminine.

EXERCISES:

1. Ella va a la iglesia todas las semanas.
2. Mis niños van a la iglesia conmigo todas las semanas.
3. ¿Van ustedes a la iglesia todas las semanas?
4. Sí, nosotros siempre vamos a la iglesia.
5. Nosotros no podemos caminar a la iglesia.
6. Ustedes cargan los libros a la escuela todos los días.
7. Yo no puedo leer el libro.
8. Mi hermano quiere agua porque tiene sed.
9. El señor Jones nunca va a la iglesia.
10. ¿Quieres el periódico hoy?

Answers on page 251.

LESSON 120

NEW WORD **biblioteca**

MEANING *library*

Biblioteca is feminine.

Remember that the word **de** can mean *of* or *from*.

EXERCISES:

1. **Yo quiero leer libros, pero no puedo ir a la biblioteca.**
2. **Mis amigos van a la biblioteca todas las semanas.**
3. **¿Quieres tú ir a la biblioteca?**
4. **¿Quiere usted ir a la biblioteca?**
5. **No, yo no quiero leer libros hoy, pero puedo ir a la biblioteca con usted mañana.**
6. **Yo quiero unos libros de la biblioteca.**
7. **Nosotros nunca vamos a la iglesia, pero necesitamos ir todas las semanas.**
8. **Mis perros no pueden leer el periódico.**
9. **Él siempre carga un periódico.**
10. **El perro tiene el periódico de mi papá.**

Answers on page 252.

LESSON 121

EXPRESSING PURPOSE

In everyday conversation, we often tell others the reason why we are doing something. Consider the following example:

I am going to the mall <u>for the purpose of buying</u> clothes.

That sentence was a little wordy, wasn't it? We could say the same thing in a shorter way, using an infinitive, like this:

I am going to the mall <u>to buy</u> clothes.

In that example, we used an infinitive to express purpose—to communicate to someone the reason for our trip to the mall. Think about this for a moment, and in the next lesson, we will study how to express purpose in Spanish.

LESSON 122

EXPRESSING PURPOSE IN SPANISH

In this lesson, we will learn how to express purpose in Spanish. To accomplish this, we will use the infinitive, accompanied by a helping word.

The two helping words that will help us express purpose are **para** and **a**. You already know the preposition **a**, which means *to*, but you have not seen the word **para** before. The word **para** is often translated into English as *for* or *to*, but keep in mind that the word **para** can be used in many different situations. In this lesson, we will be using the word **para** in a situation in which it means *for the purpose of* or *in order to*.

So the words **para** and **a** can help us to express purpose in Spanish. Let's look at these examples:

> **Yo siempre voy a la tienda <u>para comprar</u> comida.**
> **Yo siempre voy a la tienda <u>a comprar</u> comida.**

Both of these sentences mean exactly the same thing: *I always go to the store to buy food.* In each example, the speaker used an infinitive, with either **para** or **a** coming before it. It's just two ways of saying the same thing.

EXERCISES:

1. **Mis padres van a menudo al centro comercial para comprar ropa.**
2. **Él nunca va a la biblioteca a leer libros y periódicos.**
3. **Mi hija va a la biblioteca para leer libros todos los días.**
4. **Yo voy al centro comercial todas las semanas a ver a mis amigos.**
5. **Tú vas a la tienda todos los días para trabajar.**
6. **Ella siempre va al parque a caminar.**
7. **Nosotros vamos a la iglesia todas las semanas.**
8. **Ustedes no pueden comprar un carro.**
9. **Todos los días yo camino a la biblioteca para leer libros.**
10. **Ellas necesitan ir al centro comercial a comprar ropa.**

Answers on page 252.

LESSON 123

NEW WORD **restaurante**

MEANING *restaurant*

Restaurante, our new word for this lesson, is masculine.

EXERCISES:

1. Nosotros vamos al restaurante todas las semanas.
2. Yo voy al restaurante a menudo para comer con mis amigos.
3. Mi familia va al restaurante a comer todas las semanas.
4. ¿Quieres tú ir al restaurante para comer?
5. ¡Sí, yo quiero comer porque tengo hambre!
6. Nosotros no podemos ir al restaurante hoy porque no tenemos dinero.
7. Él no tiene su periódico, pero tiene sus libros.
8. Yo nunca voy a la iglesia, pero voy a mi trabajo todos los días.
9. ¿Lee usted un libro todas las semanas?
10. Sí, yo leo dos libros todas las semanas.

Answers on page 252.

LESSON 124

NEW WORDS **todas las noches**

MEANING *every night*

Also, you will want to know the expression **esta noche** which means *tonight*.

EXERCISES:

1. **Ellos van al restaurante para comer todas las noches.**
2. **Yo quiero ir al restaurante esta noche.**
3. **Las mujeres quieren ir a la iglesia esta noche.**
4. **¿Quieres tú ir a la biblioteca conmigo esta noche?**
5. **El señor Smith siempre carga el periódico al parque.**
6. **¿Podemos ir al centro comercial para comprar ropa esta noche?**
7. **No, pero tú puedes ir a la biblioteca a leer tu libro.**
8. **Nosotros no queremos ir a la iglesia esta noche.**
9. **Nosotros queremos caminar al parque todas las noches.**
10. **Él nunca va a la escuela sin sus libros.**

Answers on page 253.

LESSON 125

yo desayuno / desayunar

MEANING   *I have breakfast / to have breakfast*

Desayunar, the infinitive form, ends in **–ar**, so you know that this verb is from the first conjugation. In Spanish the word for *breakfast* (as a noun) is **desayuno**.

EXERCISES:

1. **Yo desayuno todos los días.**
2. **Mi familia desayuna todos los días.**
3. **Yo quiero desayunar, pero nosotros no tenemos comida.**
4. **¿Quieres desayunar conmigo hoy?**
5. **Tus padres van al restaurante a comer todas las noches.**
6. **Él quiere ir a un restaurante para desayunar.**
7. **Él quiere ir a un restaurante a desayunar.**
8. **Yo quiero comprar un carro, pero no tengo dinero.**
9. **Ustedes quieren desayunar porque tienen hambre.**
10. **Yo cargo comida conmigo todos los días.**

Answers on page 253.

LESSON 126

NEW WORDS **todas las mañanas**

MEANING *every morning*

You already know that the word **mañana** means *tomorrow*, but as a noun it can also mean *morning*.

In addition to **todas las mañanas**, you might also want to know how to say *this morning*, which is **esta mañana**.

EXERCISES:

1. **Yo no quiero trabajar esta mañana.**
2. **Mi familia desayuna conmigo todas las mañanas.**
3. **Mi hermana va a la escuela todas las mañanas.**
4. **Nosotros desayunamos todas las mañanas.**
5. **Yo quiero desayunar con mi familia esta mañana.**
6. **Mi padre lee el periódico todas las mañanas.**
7. **Ellos quieren ir al restaurante todas las mañanas a desayunar.**
8. **¿Va usted a la playa a menudo con su familia?**
9. **No, nosotros nunca vamos a la playa, pero vamos al parque a menudo.**
10. **Yo bebo agua todas las mañanas.**

Answers on page 253.

LESSON 127

NEW WORDS   **yo almuerzo / almorzar**

MEANING   *I have lunch / to have lunch*

PRONUNCIATION TIP: In Spanish, the letter *z* always sounds like an *s* (except in Spain).

In Spanish the word for *lunch* (as a noun) is **almuerzo**.

This verb is a stem-changing or shoe verb. Can you identify the forms that use the stem that comes from the infinitive, and the ones that have the changed stem?

	SINGULAR	PLURAL
FIRST PERSON	**yo almuerzo**	**nosotros/nosotras almorzamos**
SECOND PERSON	**tú almuerzas**	**vosotros/vosotras almorzáis** (Spain only)
THIRD PERSON	**él/ella almuerza** **usted almuerza** (used as 2nd person)	**ellos/ellas almuerzan** **ustedes almuerzan** (used as 2nd person)

EXERCISES:

1. **Mis amigos almuerzan conmigo todos los días.**
2. **¿Quieres tú almorzar conmigo?**
3. **Sí, yo quiero almorzar contigo.**
4. **Fred Smith, mi amigo, quiere almorzar conmigo hoy.**
5. **Nosotros necesitamos almorzar.**
6. **Ella desayuna con sus padres todas las mañanas.**
7. **Yo quiero ir al restaurante contigo.**
8. **Yo almuerzo con mis amigos todos los días.**

9. **Ellas quieren almorzar con Michael todos los días.**
10. **Ustedes nunca leen el periódico.**

Answers on page 254.

LESSON 128

NEW WORD **ahora**

MEANING *now*

PRONUNCIATION TIP: Remember that in Spanish, the letter *h* is always silent.

Another good expression to know is **ahora mismo**, which means *right now.*

EXERCISES:

1. **Yo quiero ir a la playa ahora.**
2. **¡Yo quiero almorzar ahora mismo porque tengo hambre!**
3. **Mis perros quieren comer ahora mismo.**
4. **Ella quiere leer su periódico ahora.**
5. **Yo quiero ir al centro comercial ahora para comprar ropa.**
6. **¿Puedes ir al centro comercial conmigo?**
7. **Nosotros leemos libros todos los días.**
8. **¿Tiene usted diez dólares?**
9. **Sí, pero yo quiero ir a la tienda para comprar comida.**
10. **Las muchachas van al restaurante todas las noches a comer.**

Answers on page 254.

LESSON 129

NEW WORDS **yo ceno / cenar**

MEANING   *I have dinner / to have dinner*

Cenar, the infinitive form, ends in **–ar**, so you know that this verb is from the first conjugation. In Spanish the word for *dinner* (as a noun) is **cena**.

Because this is a regular verb, you can create the different forms of it on your own using the infinitive form.

EXERCISES:

1. **Yo ceno con mi familia todas las noches.**
2. **Ellos van al restaurante a cenar todas las noches.**
3. **Yo no quiero almorzar; quiero cenar.**
4. **Mi hermana cena conmigo todas las semanas.**
5. **Nosotros desayunamos todas las mañanas.**
6. **Ella quiere cenar con sus amigas todas las noches.**
7. **Yo quiero cenar ahora mismo porque tengo hambre.**
8. **¿Quieres tú ir a la biblioteca para leer libros?**
9. **No, yo quiero ir a la playa.**
10. **Tú no puedes ir a la tienda porque no tienes un carro.**

Answers on page 254.

LESSON 130

TWO WAYS TO SAY "I AM"

In Spanish there are two ways to say verbs of being (also known as linking verbs). One way is used when talking about things that are permanent, and the other is used when talking about things that are temporary.

Let's think for a moment about things that are permanent. Consider the following examples:

He is my father.
The mountain is large.

In those examples, the situation being described is permanent. If someone is your father, he will always be your father. He will not be your father today, and not your father tomorrow—it's a permanent situation. Likewise, if a mountain is large, it will always be large. It will not be large today and small tomorrow. So that also is a permanent situation.

Other situations are temporary. Let's look at the following examples:

I am in the kitchen.
He is tired.

If you are in the kitchen, you can easily move from the kitchen to another room. So your location is a temporary situation. Likewise, if someone is tired, he or she could remedy that by getting a good night's sleep or perhaps by taking a nap. So that also is a temporary situation.

The verbs of being that you already know (such as **yo soy**, **tú eres** and the rest) are the verbs that we use in Spanish to talk about situations that are permanent. In the next lesson, you will learn a new set of verbs of being—special verbs of being that Spanish speakers use when talking about situations that are temporary.

LESSON 131

NEW WORDS **yo estoy / estar**

MEANING *I am / to be*

In the last lesson, we learned that **yo soy**, **tú eres** and the other verbs of being that you know are used when talking about situations that are permanent. But you also learned that in Spanish, there are special verbs of being that Spanish speakers use when talking about situations that are temporary.

Yo estoy/estar, the new word for this lesson, is the verb we use in Spanish to talk about things that are temporary. This is an irregular verb, so you just have to memorize the different forms by repetition. Here is a handy chart to help you.

	SINGULAR	PLURAL
FIRST PERSON	**yo estoy**	**nosotros/nosotras estamos**
SECOND PERSON	**tú estás**	**vosotros/vosotras estáis** (Spain only)
THIRD PERSON	**él/ella está** **usted está** (used as 2nd person)	**ellos/ellas están** **ustedes están** (used as 2nd person)

Try to familiarize yourself with these verb forms, and in the next lesson we will get some practice actually using them in sentences.

LESSON 132

NEW WORD   en

MEANING   *in, at, on*

The word **en**, which Spanish speakers use constantly, is a very flexible preposition. It can be translated into English several different ways, such as *in, at* or *on.*

Let's look at some examples of how the word **en** can be used in a sentence. Here is an example of a situation in which **en** would mean *in.*

> He is **en** the kitchen.

Here is an example of a situation in which **en** would mean *at.*

> We are **en** the beach.

Here is an example of a situation in which **en** would mean *on.*

> The cat is **en** the table.

So you see, the word **en** is really quite versatile.

When translating the exercises for this lesson, you will need to use the context of the sentence to decide exactly how to translate the word **en**. Will you translate **en** as *in, at* or *on?* Use the translation that sounds best in the context of the sentence.

Remember that when something is temporary, that is expressed using the forms of **yo estoy**, not **yo soy**. You will probably want to refer back to lesson 131 often to review the forms of **yo estoy**.

EXERCISES:

1. **Yo trabajo en un banco.**
2. **Mi hermana está en el carro.**
3. **Nosotros estamos en la biblioteca.**
4. **Yo quiero estar en la playa.**
5. **Ellos están en el parque.**

6. **Tú estás en una iglesia.**
7. **Yo estoy en el restaurante para almorzar.**
8. **Tus gatos quieren comer ahora mismo.**
9. **Nosotros necesitamos comprar comida esta noche.**
10. **Yo necesito cenar ahora.**

Answers on page 255.

LESSON 133

NEW WORDS **mesa / escritorio**

MEANING *table / desk*

Mesa, like most nouns that end with **–a**, is feminine. And **escritorio**, like most nouns that end with **–o**, is masculine.

Remember that **en** can mean *in, at* or *on*.

EXERCISES:

1. **El periódico de mi padre está en el escritorio.**
2. **¡Los gatos están en la mesa!**
3. **La comida no está en la mesa, pero nosotros queremos cenar.**
4. **Tus amigos están en la playa, pero tú estás en la biblioteca.**
5. **Mi familia está en el parque ahora.**
6. **Nosotros estamos en un restaurante porque queremos almorzar.**
7. **¿Tiene usted un perro?**
8. **No, pero yo tengo unos gatos.**
9. **Ustedes son mis amigos.**
10. **Él es mi padre.**

Answers on page 255.

LESSON 134

NEW WORD **casa**

MEANING *house*

Casa, the new word for this lesson, is feminine.

EXERCISES:

1. **Mis niños están en la casa ahora.**
2. **Mi gato no está en la casa.**
3. **Los gatos están en la casa.**
4. **El gato está en la mesa y quiere mi comida.**
5. **Yo cargo mis libros a menudo porque quiero leer.**
6. **Mi mamá tiene hambre y quiere cenar ahora mismo.**
7. **Los muchachos van al restaurante a comer todas las noches.**
8. **Nosotros estamos en la playa.**
9. **Mi padre quiere leer el periódico, pero el periódico no está en el escritorio.**
10. **¿Quieres tú cenar en un restaurante?**

Answers on page 255.

LESSON 135

NEW WORDS   **cocina / comedor / sala**

MEANING   *kitchen / dining room / living room*

In this book we usually only learn one new word per lesson. But for this lesson, you will need to memorize three new words!

Cocina, which means *kitchen*, is feminine. So is **sala**, which means *living room*. But **comedor**, which means *dining room*, is masculine.

Here's a helpful rule to know: All nouns ending in **–dor** are masculine (like **comedor**).

EXERCISES:

1. **La comida está en la cocina.**
2. **La mesa está en el comedor.**
3. **El periódico está en la sala.**
4. **Los niños están en la sala.**
5. **Sin una mesa, nosotros no podemos cenar.**
6. **Yo estoy en la casa.**
7. **Tú siempre estás en la biblioteca, pero nunca lees los libros.**
8. **Mi papá quiere su periódico, pero no está en su escritorio.**
9. **Mi familia desayuna todas las mañanas.**
10. **Mi madre está en el comedor, pero no quiere cenar porque no tiene hambre.**

Answers on page 256.

LESSON 136

NEW WORDS **habitación / cama**

MEANING *bedroom / bed*

PRONUNCIATION TIP: Remember that in Spanish, the letter *h* is always silent.

Both **habitación** and **cama** are feminine.

Here's a helpful rule to know: All nouns ending in **–ción** are feminine (like **habitación**).

EXERCISES:

1. **Mi hermana está en su habitación.**
2. **Los gatos están en mi cama.**
3. **¿Están los niños en la cama?**
4. **Los perros están en la cama con mis padres.**
5. **Mi cama y mi escritorio están en mi habitación.**
6. **Mis hermanos y hermanas están en la casa.**
7. **Tus padres están en la sala, pero tu hermano está en la cocina porque él tiene hambre.**
8. **Nosotros queremos ir al comedor porque queremos cenar ahora.**
9. **Yo estoy en mi cama porque no puedo trabajar hoy.**
10. **El gato está en la mesa.**

Answers on page 256.

LESSON 137

THE GERUND

The time has come for us to learn about an important Spanish verb form called the *gerund*. We translate a Spanish gerund into English with words that end in *–ing*, such as *walking*, *talking*, and *eating*.

Let's learn how to make a Spanish gerund. First, let's see how to do it with verbs of the first conjugation (verbs whose infinitives end in **–ar**). Let's practice with the verb **comprar**.

First, take the infinitive form of the verb:

comprar

Then, remove the **–ar** from the end of the word:

compr-

Now, add the ending **–ando**:

compr<u>ando</u>

That leaves you with the gerund form, which is **comprando. Comprando** means *buying*.

Now, let's learn how to make a gerund from a second conjugation verb (a verb whose infinitive ends in **–er**). Let's practice with the verb **comer**.

First, take the infinitive form of the verb:

comer

Then, remove the **–er** from the end of the word:

com-

Now, add the ending **–iendo**:

com<u>iendo</u>

That leaves you with the gerund form, which is **comiendo**. **Comiendo** means *eating*.

For verbs of the third conjugation, the process is almost exactly like the second conjugation. But don't worry about that right now—we can discuss that later if needed. Also, there are a few gerund forms that are irregular, and we will discuss those as needed, too.

In the next lesson, we will use the gerund in actual sentences. But in the meantime, try to make each of the following infinitives into gerunds. To do that, you will need to figure out what conjugation the verb is from, and then make the appropriate changes to the ending, as seen in the instructions above.

EXERCISES:

1. **trabajar**
2. **hablar**
3. **desayunar**
4. **comer**
5. **beber**
6. **ver**
7. **caminar**
8. **tener**

Answers on page 256.

LESSON 138

USING THE GERUND

We already know how to say *I buy* in Spanish. Its easy—you just say **yo compro**. But to say *I am buying*, you need to use a gerund. Let's use a gerund in an actual sentence. Consider the following example:

> **Yo estoy comprando.**

This sentence means *I am buying*. Notice that we had **yo estoy** (the verb of being used for temporary things) followed by a gerund. When using a gerund, the **estoy** verbs are the only verbs you may use. In other words, you would never say **yo soy comprando**.

Let's look at another example, this time using the verb **yo como/comer**.

> **Él está comiendo.**

This sentence means *He is eating*. Again, we have the verb of being used for temporary things followed by a gerund.

It doesn't matter if the subject of the sentence is masculine, feminine, singular or plural—the gerund is always the same. So gerunds are easy to understand and use.

Now try these simple exercises, and if you get stuck you can always check the answer key in the back of the book.

EXERCISES:

1. **Yo estoy comprando.**
2. **Tú estás comiendo.**
3. **Él está comiendo en la sala.**
4. **Ella está comprando un carro.**
5. **Nosotros no estamos comiendo.**
6. **¿Están ustedes comiendo en la sala?**
7. **Ellos están comiendo en la cocina.**
8. **Ellas están comprando ropa.**

9. **Nosotros podemos comer en el comedor.**
10. **El perro está en la habitación en la cama.**

Answers on page 257.

NEW WORDS   **yo cocino / cocinar / cocinando**

MEANING   *I cook / to cook / cooking*

Cocinar, the infinitive form, ends in **–ar**, so you know that this verb is from the first conjugation.

Watch out for any word that ends in **–ando** or **–iendo**. If a word has one of those endings, it's definitely a gerund!

EXERCISES:

1. **Yo estoy cocinando en la cocina.**
2. **Tú estás cocinando la comida.**
3. **Mi hermano quiere cocinar la cena todas las noches.**
4. **Yo cocino todas las noches, pero esta noche yo quiero ir a un restaurante a cenar.**
5. **Ellos tienen hambre porque nunca desayunan.**
6. **Tu comida no está en la mesa; está en el escritorio.**
7. **Nosotros estamos en la sala.**
8. **Ella cocina todas las noches.**
9. **Él no puede cocinar hoy; necesitamos almorzar en un restaurante.**
10. **Mi cama está en mi habitación.**

Answers on page 257.

LESSON 140

NEW WORDS   **yo hago / hacer / haciendo**

MEANING   *I do, I make / to do, to make / doing, making*

PRONUNCIATION TIP: Remember that in Spanish, the letter h is always silent. So **hago** will sound similar to *AH-go*.

This verb can mean *do* or *make*. You must use the context of the sentence to determine the best translation.

Hacer, the infinitive form, ends in **–er** so you know that this verb is from the second conjugation. It's a fairly regular verb, except for the first person singular, which has a *g* instead of a *c*.

Familiarize yourself with the different forms of **yo hago/hacer** with this handy chart.

	SINGULAR	PLURAL
FIRST PERSON	**yo hago**	**nosotros/nosotras hacemos**
SECOND PERSON	**tú haces**	**vosotros/vosotras hacéis** (Spain only)
THIRD PERSON	**él/ella hace** **usted hace** (used as 2nd person)	**ellos/ellas hacen** **ustedes hacen** (used as 2nd person)

Before you start the exercises, let's review the names of the three daily meals:

Breakfast is the masculine word **desayuno**.
Lunch is the masculine word **almuerzo**.
Dinner is the feminine word **cena**.

Okay, now let's give these exercises a try.

EXERCISES:

1. **Yo estoy haciendo la cena.**
2. **Ella hace el almuerzo todos los días.**
3. **Él va a la biblioteca todos los días a hacer su trabajo.**
4. **Nosotros estamos haciendo el desayuno ahora mismo.**
5. **Yo desayuno todas las mañanas, pero tú nunca desayunas.**
6. **Ellas siempre hacen la cena.**
7. **¿Haces tú el desayuno todas las mañanas?**
8. **Yo siempre hago mi trabajo.**
9. **Él está cocinando la comida en la cocina, pero yo estoy en mi habitación.**
10. **Yo estoy cenando en mi habitación esta noche.**

Answers on page 257.

LESSON 141

NEW WORD **para**

MEANING *for*

Let's talk a little more about the word **para**. The word **para** is often translated into English as *for* or *to*, but the word **para** can have different shades of meaning in different contexts. We have already used the word **para** to help us express purpose, as seen in this example:

> **Yo voy a la biblioteca <u>para</u> leer libros a menudo** *(I go to the library to read books often).*

In that example, **para** meant something like *for the purpose of* or *in order to*, even though we did not translate it in either of those ways. But **para** can also mean *for* in the sense of *intended for*, as seen in this example:

> **Yo quiero hacer almuerzo para mis padres hoy** *(I want to make lunch for my parents today).*

In that example, the speaker said that he wanted to make lunch *for* his parents, in the sense that the lunch was *intended for* his parents. So when you see the word **para**, think about the following possibilities:

- Expressing purpose
- Expressing intended recipient

Check the answers in the back if you get stuck.

EXERCISES:

1. **Yo quiero hacer almuerzo para mis amigos.**
2. **Mi padre no quiere comprar un carro para mi hermano.**
3. **Mis padres van a la tienda para comprar comida todas las semanas.**
4. **Nosotros estamos comprando un perro para los niños.**
5. **Yo hago comida para mis amigos todas las semanas.**
6. **Tú haces comida para tus perros todos los días.**
7. **Mi hermano está haciendo la cena para sus niños.**

169

8. **Mi madre está cocinando la comida ahora mismo.**
9. **Los niños están en la cama ahora.**
10. **Yo siempre cargo libros y voy a la biblioteca para leer todos los días.**

Answers on page 258.

LESSON 142

NEW WORDS **yo duermo / dormir / durmiendo**

MEANING *I sleep / to sleep / sleeping*

You can tell that this verb is from the third conjugation because **dormir**, the infinitive form, ends in **–ir**.

This is a stem-changing verb, or shoe verb. That means that the first person plural and second person plural forms will be based on the stem taken from the infinitive, but the other forms will have an altered stem.

Use this handy chart to familiarize yourself with the different forms of **yo duermo**.

	SINGULAR	PLURAL
FIRST PERSON	**yo duermo**	**nosotros/nosotras dormimos**
SECOND PERSON	**tú duermes**	**vosotros/vosotras dormís** (Spain only)
THIRD PERSON	**él/ella duerme** **usted duerme** (used as 2nd person)	**ellos/ellas duermen** **ustedes duermen** (used as 2nd person)

And, no lesson on a shoe verb would be complete without the chance to draw a shoe. So get out your pens and pencils and draw your best shoe on the chart on the next page.

duermo	dormimos
duermes	dormís
duerme	duermen

EXERCISES:

1. Yo duermo en mi cama todas las noches.
2. Ella está durmiendo en su cama con sus gatos.
3. El gato duerme en la sala todas las noches.
4. Yo no quiero ir a la playa; yo quiero dormir en mi cama.
5. Los niños están durmiendo.
6. Ella está cocinando la comida para su familia.
7. Nosotros no podemos ir al parque porque estamos almorzando ahora mismo.
8. ¿Tiene usted un escritorio en su habitación?
9. No, pero yo tengo una mesa en mi sala.
10. Mi madre está haciendo la cena ahora mismo; ella hace la cena todas las noches.

Answers on page 258.

LESSON 143

NEW WORD **hay**

MEANING *there is, there are*

PRONUNCIATION TIP: The word **hay** sounds like the English word *eye*.

Sometimes, in conversation, we just want to say *there is*. In Spanish we do that by using the word **hay**. This is very easy to do. Here is an example:

Hay un gato en la casa *(There is a cat in the house).*

Even if the thing you are talking about is plural, you still use the same word, **hay**, like this:

Hay tres gatos en la casa *(There are three cats in the house).*

See how easy that was? Now get to work on these exercises.

EXERCISES:

1. **Hay un perro en la casa.**
2. **Hay dos escritorios en mi habitación.**
3. **Hay unos niños en el parque.**
4. **Hay un gato en la mesa.**
5. **Hay comida en la cocina.**
6. **Los niños están durmiendo en la cama.**
7. **¡Yo necesito comer ahora mismo!**
8. **Yo siempre hago mi trabajo.**
9. **Todas las noches mi gato va a mi habitación para dormir en la cama conmigo.**
10. **Mis hijos quieren cocinar la cena esta noche.**

Answers on page 258.

LESSON 144

HOW TO SAY THAT YOU LIKE SOMETHING

In everyday conversation, we are constantly saying either that we like things, or that we do not like things. So it's time for us to learn how to make this type of statement in Spanish.

But it's a little complicated. In Spanish, when you say you like something, the sentence structure is different than it would be in English. Let's compare the sentence structure of this type of sentence in English, and a similar Spanish sentence. First, the English:

> I like the beach.

In that sentence, the subject was the word *I*, and the word *like* was the verb. The word *beach* was the target or recipient of the action, or what in technical terms we would call the *direct object*.

Now let's take a look at how that same sentence would be structured in Spanish:

> The beach is pleasing to me.

As you can see, in this sentence, everything is reversed. The word *beach* is now the subject of the sentence instead of being the direct object. Likewise, instead of the speaker being the subject, the speaker (me) is the one being pleased by the beach. And the verb is not to *like*, but to *be pleasing*.

So here is the bottom line: In English, we say that *we like something*, but in Spanish we say that *something is pleasing to us*.

This type of Spanish sentence is an idiom. In other words, we don't translate it into English literally. A Spanish sentence might literally say *The beach is pleasing to me*, but we would still translate that sentence into English as *I like the beach*.

Give this some thought, and in the next few lessons, we will learn the actual Spanish words needed to make these kinds of statements.

LESSON 145

NEW WORD **gustar**

MEANING *to be pleasing*

In the last lesson, we learned that in English you would say *I like the beach*, but in Spanish you would literally say *The beach is pleasing to me.*

So we need to learn the Spanish verb that means *to be pleasing*. Let's examine the following chart:

	SINGULAR	PLURAL
FIRST PERSON	(unnecessary)	(unnecessary)
SECOND PERSON	(unnecessary)	(unnecessary)
THIRD PERSON	gusta	gustan

Gustar (that's the infinitive form), our new verb for this lesson, is a regular verb of the first conjugation. But we won't be needing all the forms of this verb. In fact, the only forms of this verb that we will study in this book are the third person singular and the third person plural (these two forms are circled in the chart). **Gusta**, because it is third person and singular, means *he is pleasing, she is pleasing*, or *it is pleasing*. Also, in the context of formal speech, **gusta** could mean *you are pleasing*. **Gustan**, because it is third person and plural, means *they are pleasing*. Also, in the context of formal speech, **gustan** could mean *y'all are pleasing* (also in everyday speech in the Americas). So you see, **gusta** is singular, and **gustan** is plural.

So let's see if we can figure out how to use **gusta** and **gustan** in actual sentences. Let's revisit our English sentence example from the last lesson:

I like the beach.

Now, imagine that you want to say it in Spanish. In Spanish, you would literally say something like this:

The beach is pleasing to me.

If that sentence were in Spanish, the speaker would need to use the word **gusta**, which is singular. Since *the beach* is singular, **gusta** is the appropriate verb to use in this situation.

But what if you wanted to say that you like more than one thing? Consider the following example:

I like cats.

Now, imagine that you want to say it in Spanish. In Spanish, you would literally say something like this:

Cats are pleasing to me.

If that sentence were in Spanish, the speaker would need to use the word **gustan**, which is plural. Since the word *cats* is plural, **gustan** is the appropriate verb to use in this situation.

So, here is the bottom line: If the thing being liked is singular, you will need to use **gusta**, the singular form. If the thing being liked is plural, you will need to use **gustan**, the plural form.

LESSON 146

TO WHOM IS IT PLEASING?

In the last lesson, we learned that we can use the third person singular verb **gusta** to say that one thing is pleasing, and that we can use the third person plural verb **gustan** to say that more than one thing is pleasing.

But there is one last ingredient that we need! Consider the following example:

> **Me gusta.**

Literally, **me gusta** means *It is pleasing to me*. But we translate it simply as *I like it*. So you see, the word **me**, (which means *to me*) is extremely important here. That word tells you who is being pleased. So let's make a complete sentence with **me gusta**:

> **Me gusta la playa.**

Notice how the **me gusta** part of the sentence comes first, and the thing being liked comes afterward. Translated literally, that example sentence would say *To me is pleasing the beach*. But we translate it into English as *I like the beach*.

Now let's learn how to say *You like the beach*:

> **Te gusta la playa.**

The key word here is **te**, which means *to you*. Translated literally, that example sentence would say *To you is pleasing the beach*. But we translate it into English as *You like the beach*.

Let's look at another one:

> **Le gusta la playa.**

The word **le** can mean *to him*, *to her*, or *to it*. Translated literally, that example sentence could possibly say *To him is pleasing the beach, To her is pleasing the beach,* or *To it is pleasing the beach*. And of course, we would translate them into English as *He likes the beach, She likes the beach,* or *It likes the beach*.

177

By now, you should be getting the idea about how to use **me gusta**. To make full use of **me gusta**, you will need to know a total of six different words like **me**, **te** and **le**. Let's examine a chart of all these special words so that you can easily familiarize yourself with them.

	SINGULAR	PLURAL
FIRST PERSON	**me** *(to me)*	**nos** *(to us)*
SECOND PERSON	**te** *(to you)*	**os** *(to y'all)* (Spain only)
THIRD PERSON	**le** *(to him, to her, to it)* (used as 2nd person: *to you*)	**les** *(to them)* (used as 2nd person: *to y'all*)

So, to say that somebody likes something, just insert the appropriate word (**me**, **te**, **le**, **nos**, **os**, or **les**.) Remember that if the thing being liked is plural, you need to use the plural verb **gustan** instead of the singular verb **gusta**.

To help you get accustomed to using the different forms of **me gusta**, we have provided a chart on the next page. Take a few minutes to practice with it. Keep practicing until you feel comfortable with each of the different sentences.

SPANISH	SEMI-LITERAL TRANSLATION	TRANSLATION
Me gusta la playa. **Me gustan los gatos.**	*The beach is pleasing to me.* *Cats are pleasing to me.*	*I like the beach.* *I like cats.*
Te gusta la playa. **Te gustan los gatos.**	*The beach is pleasing to you.* *Cats are pleasing to you.*	*You like the beach.* *You like cats.*
Le gusta la playa. **Le gustan los gatos.**	*The beach is pleasing to him, her or it.* (Formal speech: *The beach is pleasing to you.)* *Cats are pleasing to him, her or it.* (Formal speech: *Cats are pleasing to you.)*	*He, she or it likes the beach.* (Formal speech: *You like the beach.)* *He, she or it likes cats.* (Formal speech: *You like cats.)*
Nos gusta la playa. **Nos gustan los gatos.**	*The beach is pleasing to us.* *Cats are pleasing to us.*	*We like the beach.* *We like cats.*
Os gusta la playa. **Os gustan los gatos.**	*The beach is pleasing to y'all.* *Cats are pleasing to y'all.*	*Y'all like the beach.* *Y'all like cats.*
Les gusta la playa. **Les gustan los gatos.**	*The beach is pleasing to them.* (Formal speech in Spain or everyday speech in the Americas: *The beach is pleasing to y'all.)* *Cats are pleasing to them.* (Formal speech in Spain or everyday speech in the Americas: *Cats are pleasing to y'all.)*	*They like the beach.* (Formal speech in Spain or everyday speech in the Americas: *Y'all like the beach.)* *They like cats.* (Formal speech in Spain or everyday speech in the Americas: *Y'all like cats.)*

LESSON 147

I DON'T LIKE IT!

Now, after much effort, we know how to say that we like things. But how do you say that you don't like something? Don't worry, because it's very easy. Just insert the word **no** before **me gusta**, as seen in the following example:

No me gusta la playa (*I do not like the beach*).

So everything is the same as before, but with the word **no** thrown in.

EXERCISES:

1. **No me gusta mi comida.**
2. **No me gustan los gatos de mi madre.**
3. **No te gusta la comida.**
4. **No te gustan los gatos.**
5. **Le gusta la playa.**
6. **Yo no puedo dormir porque no me gusta la cama.**
7. **Nos gusta el restaurante, pero no tenemos hambre.**
8. **Hay unos muchachos en la playa.**
9. **Les gusta el libro.**
10. **Yo estoy haciendo mi trabajo, pero tú siempre estás durmiendo.**

Answers on page 259.

LESSON 148

CLARIFYING THE "ME GUSTA" SENTENCE

A couple of lessons ago, we learned that the word **le** can mean *to him, to her* or *to it* (or, in the context of formal speech, *to you)*. Here's an example of that.

Le gusta la playa.

This sentence could mean *He likes the beach, She likes the beach,* or *It likes the beach* (or, in formal speech, *You like the beach)*. How do you know which one it's supposed to be?

In actual conversations, Spanish speakers often clarify sentences like this with the preposition **a** which means *to*. With the preposition **a**, you could say things like this:

A papá *(to Dad)*
A mamá *(to Mom)*
Al hombre *(to the man)*

Let's add these to a sentence and see how they can help clarify things. Here's an example:

A papá le gusta la playa *(Dad likes the beach)*.

Translated literally, that sentence would mean *To Dad to him is pleasing the beach.* It's helpful for us to have the words **a papá** here in our sentence because those words let us know that the word **le** is referring to *Dad.* But we would translate it into English as *Dad likes the beach.* Here is another example:

A mamá le gustan los gatos *(Mom likes cats)*.

Again, translated literally, that sentence would mean *To Mom to her are pleasing the cats.* It's helpful for us to have the words **a mamá** here in our sentence, because those words let us know that the word **le** is referring to *Mom.* But we would translate it into English as *Mom likes cats.*

Using the preposition **a** to clarify the sentence works with **les** too, as seen in this example:

A los gatos les gusta la comida *(The cats like the food).*

This one, translated literally, would mean *To the cats to them is pleasing the food.* It's helpful for us to have the words **a los gatos** here in our sentence, because those words let us know that the word **les** is referring to *the cats*. But we would translate it into English as *The cats like the food.*

Once you think you understand how this works, try to translate the exercises. Check the answer key in the back of the book if you get stuck.

EXERCISES:

1. **A la muchacha le gusta la comida.**
2. **A tu padre le gustan los libros.**
3. **A los hombres les gusta la comida.**
4. **No me gusta el parque.**
5. **A papá le gusta el carro de su amigo.**
6. **A las muchachas les gusta el centro comercial.**
7. **A tu familia le gusta la playa.**
8. **Yo hago la cena todas las noches, pero tú siempre estás durmiendo en tu habitación.**
9. **Me gusta cocinar.**
10. **Hay unos libros en tu escritorio.**

Answers on page 259.

L E S S O N   1 4 9

USING PRONOUNS TO CLARIFY THE "ME GUSTA" SENTENCE

In the past couple of lessons, we have learned that **le** and **les** often need to be clarified. In order to do that, we used the preposition **a** to demonstrate who or what is meant by **le** and **les**.

But you can also use pronouns like **él** and **ella** to clarify a **me gusta** type sentence, like this:

> **A él le gusta la comida.**

That example, translated literally, means *To him to him is pleasing the food.* So having the words **a él** at the beginning of the sentence is helpful because they tell us whether **le** means *to him, to her,* or *to it* (or, in the context of formal speech, *to you).*

Él and **ella** are not the only pronouns you can use in this way. You may clarify your sentence with any of the following:

	SINGULAR	PLURAL
FIRST PERSON	**a mí** *(to me)*	**a nosotros/nosotras** *(to us)*
SECOND PERSON	**a ti** *(to you)*	**a vosotros/vosotras** *(to y'all)* (Spain only)
THIRD PERSON	**a él/a ella** *(to him, to her, to it)* **a usted** *(to you)*(formal)	**a ellos/a ellas** *(to them)* **a ustedes** *(to y'all)* (The Americas: for everyone; in Spain: formal)

You may be asking yourself the question, "Isn't this somewhat redundant? After all, in most sentences of this type you already know whom the sentence is talking about." Well, you do have a good point. But in real-life conversations, there are many situations in which you might need to clarify these types of sentences using the pronouns seen in the chart shown above.

Remember that when you use **usted** and **ustedes** you will use third person words such as **le** and **les**, as seen in these examples:

> **A usted le gusta la comida** *(You like the food)*.
> **A ustedes les gusta la comida** *(Y'all like the food)*.

Take the time to familiarize yourself with contents of the chart, and then give the exercises a try.

EXERCISES:

1. **A mí me gusta la comida.**
2. **A ti te gustan los perros.**
3. **A usted le gusta la playa.**
4. **A ella le gusta el restaurante.**
5. **A nosotros nos gustan los gatos.**
6. **A ustedes no les gusta mi carro.**
7. **A ellos les gusta el centro comercial.**
8. **Mi padre está haciendo su almuerzo.**
9. **Hay un gato en mi habitación y está durmiendo en mi cama.**
10. **Mi padre hace su trabajo todos los días.**

Answers on page 259.

L E S S O N   1 5 0

ASKING QUESTIONS WITH ME GUSTA

Asking whether or not someone likes something is very easy. In fact, all you do is add a question mark! Here's an example:

¿A ti te gustan los gatos? *(Do you like cats?)*

See how easy that was?

Actually, there is one thing we ought to show you. When asking a **me gusta** type question, the speaker might not say the clarifying part of the sentence until later in the sentence. So instead of this:

¿<u>A ti</u> te gustan los gatos?

You could have this:

¿Te gustan los gatos <u>a ti</u>?

Or this:

¿Te gustan <u>a ti</u> los gatos?

That's really all there is to it. So take a whack at some of these exercises.

EXERCISES:

1. **¿A ella le gusta mi carro?**
2. **¿Le gusta mi carro a ella?**
3. **¿A ellos les gusta desayunar todas las mañanas?**
4. **¿Les gusta almorzar a ellos todos los días?**
5. **¿A ti te gustan mis libros?**
6. **¿Te gusta a ti ir al centro comercial?**
7. **¿Les gusta cocinar a ellas?**
8. **A nosotros nos gusta ir a la playa.**
9. **Yo estoy cocinando la cena en la cocina.**
10. **Nosotros a menudo cargamos dinero.**

Answers on page 260.

LESSON 151

NEW IDIOM **me encanta**

MEANING *I love it*

Over the last few lessons, we have worked pretty hard to learn all the rules for using **me gusta**. It was a lot of effort, but we had to do it because learning how to use **me gusta** is a must for any student of Spanish.

Now that you know how to use **me gusta**, I have some good news for you. There are several other verbs that follow the same exact patterns of usage as **me gusta**. Our new verb for this lesson, **me encanta**, is one of those verbs.

Literally, **me encanta** means *it enchants me*. But as an idiom we translate it into English as *I love it*.

The way we use **me encanta** in a sentence is exactly the same as **me gusta**. Let's use **me encanta** in a sentence.

> **Me encanta el parque** *(I love the park)*.

Or, if the thing being loved is plural, you would use the plural form of the verb, **encantan**, as seen in this example.

> **Me encantan los gatos** *(I love cats)*.

Also, to clarify the sentence, you may use all the clarifying pronouns we studied with **me gusta**.

> **A él le encanta el restaurante** *(He loves the restaurant)*.

EXERCISES:

1. **A mí me encanta la playa.**
2. **A mi padre le encanta mi casa.**
3. **A mí me encanta cenar con mi familia.**
4. **A ti te encanta cenar todas las noches en un restaurante.**
5. **A ella le encanta comprar ropa en el centro comercial.**

186

6. **Les encanta ir a la playa a menudo.**
7. **¿Les gusta cocinar a ellos?**
8. **A ti no te gusta comer en restaurantes.**
9. **¿Hay comida en tu cocina?**
10. **¿Puedes tú trabajar hoy?**

Answers on page 260.

LESSON 152

NEW WORD **huevo**

MEANING *egg*

The word **huevo** is masculine.

You have already seen many sentences like this:

Yo quiero desayunar *(I want to have breakfast).*

But you can also use the verb **desayunar** with the names of foods, like this:

Yo quiero desayunar huevos.

We would translate this sentence into English as *I want to have eggs for breakfast.* Notice that the food being eaten for breakfast came after the word **desayunar**.

You will see this same type of sentence structure with other verbs of eating such as **almorzar** and **cenar**.

EXERCISES:

1. **A mí me encanta comer huevos.**
2. **A mi mamá le gusta cocinar huevos.**
3. **A ustedes les encanta desayunar huevos.**
4. **¿Están los huevos en la cocina?**
5. **Nosotros necesitamos comprar unos huevos mañana.**
6. **A ellos les encantan los huevos.**
7. **A él le encanta la comida de mi madre.**
8. **Nosotros no podemos ir al centro comercial porque estamos almorzando ahora.**
9. **Hay un huevo en la mesa.**
10. **Tú no puedes dormir porque no te gusta la cama.**

Answers on page 260.

LESSON 153

NEW WORDS **por favor**

MEANING *please*

EXERCISES:

1. **Yo quiero huevos, por favor.**
2. **Nosotros queremos comer ahora, por favor.**
3. **¿Puedes hacer desayuno para mí, por favor?**
4. **A mí me gusta estar en la biblioteca.**
5. **A ellos les gusta ir a la playa todas las semanas.**
6. **¿A ustedes les gusta comer huevos?**
7. **A ellos les gusta leer los libros de mi padre a menudo.**
8. **Yo necesito hacer desayuno para mis niños ahora.**
9. **A mí me encanta el parque. ¿A ti te gusta el parque también?**
10. **El perro quiere mi cena.**

Answers on page 261.

LESSON 154

NEW WORD **más**

MEANING *more*

EXERCISES:

1. **Más agua, por favor.**
2. **Hay más comida en la cocina.**
3. **Quiero más huevos, por favor.**
4. **¿Por favor, puedes tú cocinar más huevos?**
5. **A nosotros nos encanta la comida de tu madre.**
6. **Ustedes necesitan leer más libros.**
7. **Mi hermano necesita beber más agua.**
8. **El gato está en la cocina y está durmiendo en la mesa.**
9. **Yo también quiero almorzar.**
10. **Mi madre está haciendo la cena para mi padre.**

Answers on page 261.

LESSON 155

NEW WORD **gracias**

MEANING *thank you*

You already know about the word **para**, and that **para** means *for* or *in order to*. But if you want to thank someone for something specific, you don't use the word **para**. Instead, you use another Spanish word that means *for*, and that word is **por**. Here is an example of how you can use the words **gracias** and **por** to thank someone for something:

> **Gracias por la comida** *(Thank you for the food).*

One of the many challenges of learning Spanish is remembering when to use **para** and when to use **por**. And again, this is one of those things that gets easier with practice.

As long as you are learning how to say *thank you* in Spanish, you might also want to learn how to say *you're welcome*. One of the most common ways to say *you're welcome* in Spanish is **de nada**.

EXERCISES:

1. **Gracias.**
2. **De nada.**
3. **Gracias por la comida, mamá.**
4. **De nada, mi hijo.**
5. **Gracias por la ropa, papá.**
6. **De nada, mi hija.**
7. **Nosotros necesitamos más comida, por favor.**
8. **A mis hermanas no les gustan los huevos.**
9. **¿A ti te gustan los huevos?**
10. **No, a mí no me gustan los huevos.**

Answers on page 261.

LESSON 156

THANKING PEOPLE FOR DOING THINGS

If someone cooked you a tasty breakfast, you might want to thank that person by saying *Thank you for making breakfast.*

In Spanish, to thank someone for doing something, we use the word **por**, which means *for*, and an infinitive, like this:

Gracias por hacer desayuno *(Thank you for making breakfast).*

If we were to make this type of statement in English, we would use the word *making.* Therefore, an English speaker might be tempted to make the common mistake shown in this example:

Gracias por haciendo desayuno *(Thank you for making breakfast).*

It is easy to understand why an English speaker would make this kind of mistake; after all, that's the way we would construct the sentence in English. If you did say this sentence that way, a Spanish speaker would understand you, but it is still grammatically incorrect. So remember to use the infinitive in situations like this.

Here is a little rule to help you in this area: Always use an infinitive, not a gerund, after a preposition.

EXERCISES:

1. **Gracias por hacer desayuno, mamá.**
2. **Gracias por caminar a la playa conmigo.**
3. **Gracias por hacer comida para mis amigos.**
4. **Gracias por ir a la tienda y comprar la comida.**
5. **Por favor, necesito más agua.**
6. **A mi perro le encanta dormir en mi cama.**
7. **A nosotros nos encanta comer en restaurantes.**
8. **Queremos dormir ahora mismo.**
9. **Tú no puedes dormir porque tus perros y tus gatos duermen en la cama contigo todas las noches.**
10. **A él le encanta su escritorio.**

Answers on page 262.

LESSON 157

NEW WORDS   **cereal / leche**

MEANING   *cereal / milk*

PRONUNCIATION TIP: **Cereal** has three syllables, and the accent is on the last syllable.

Speaking of breakfast, in the next few lessons, we are going to learn the names of some foods you might eat to start your day. Breakfast is, after all, the most important meal of the day.

Cereal is masculine, and **leche** is feminine.

EXERCISES:

1. **Gracias por el cereal.**
2. **Queremos cereal con leche.**
3. **Yo quiero desayunar cereal con leche, por favor.**
4. **A mí me encanta la leche con mi cereal.**
5. **Hay cereal en la cocina.**
6. **¿Quieren ustedes beber leche?**
7. **Gracias por hacer mi almuerzo, papá.**
8. **A mi hermano no le gustan los huevos, pero le gusta el cereal con leche.**
9. **¿Está usted desayunando ahora mismo?**
10. **Yo no puedo cargar los libros a la escuela todas las mañanas.**

Answers on page 262.

LESSON 158

NEW WORDS   **tostada / mantequilla**

MEANING   *toast / butter*

If you are referring to one piece of *toast*, you would call it **una tostada**. But if you are referring to *toast* in a general way, you would use the plural form of **tostada** which is **tostadas**. But either way, you would probably translate it into English simply as *toast*.

Tostada and **mantequilla** are both feminine.

EXERCISES:

1. **¿Quieres tú tostadas con mantequilla?**
2. **A mí me gustan mis tostadas sin mantequilla.**
3. **Quiero más tostadas, por favor.**
4. **Gracias por hacer mis tostadas, mamá.**
5. **Yo no quiero cereal; quiero tostadas con mantequilla, por favor.**
6. **¿Quieren ustedes más leche?**
7. **A mí me encanta desayunar tostadas con mantequilla todas las mañanas.**
8. **A ellos les gusta comer huevos y tostadas todas las mañanas.**
9. **Gracias por trabajar todos los días, papá.**
10. **Ustedes no pueden comprar ropa en el centro comercial sin dinero.**

Answers on page 262.

LESSON 159

NEW WORDS **jugo / café**

MEANING   *juice / coffee*

Jugo and **café** are both masculine.

EXERCISES:

1. **Ella quiere café, pero yo quiero jugo.**
2. **Más jugo, por favor.**
3. **Gracias por hacer el café.**
4. **Mi padre está haciendo café para mi madre.**
5. **Yo no puedo dormir porque estoy bebiendo café.**
6. **A mí me encanta beber café con mi desayuno.**
7. **Nosotros bebemos café todas las mañanas.**
8. **Nosotros queremos desayunar huevos, cereal, leche y tostadas con mantequilla.**
9. **Mi papá hace el desayuno todas las mañanas; está haciendo el desayuno ahora mismo.**
10. **¿A usted le gusta su café con leche?**

Answers on page 263.

LESSON 160

NEW WORDS   **fruta / naranja**

MEANING   *fruit / orange*

The word **fruta** is somewhat similar to **tostada** because when you are referring to *fruit* in a general way, you would use the plural form of **fruta** which is **frutas**.

Fruta and **naranja** are both feminine.

EXERCISES:

1. **Nosotros necesitamos comer más frutas todos los días.**
2. **A mi hermano no le gusta comer naranjas.**
3. **¿Quieren ustedes más frutas?**
4. **Las naranjas están en la cocina en la mesa.**
5. **A mis niños les encanta comer naranjas.**
6. **Nosotros no necesitamos dormir ahora mismo; necesitamos beber café porque necesitamos trabajar.**
7. **Gracias por el cereal y las tostadas.**
8. **A mi hijo le gustan las tostadas con mantequilla.**
9. **Yo no puedo beber leche, pero a mí me encanta el jugo.**
10. **Mis amigos están caminando al parque.**

Answers on page 263.

LESSON 161

MORE ABOUT DE

By now, you have become accustomed to using the preposition **de** in two ways. We first learned that **de** is used in Spanish to show possession. Then we learned that often, **de** can simply mean *from*.

But there is another very common way that **de** is used in Spanish which we will examine in this lesson. Let's start with an example in English:

orange juice

In this example, we have two nouns next to one another. The first noun, *orange*, is telling us something about the noun that comes after it. In this case the word *orange* is telling us what the *juice* is made of.

But in Spanish, to say *orange juice*, you would not word it the same way as we would in English. In other words, you would not say **naranja jugo**. Instead, you would use the word **de**, as seen in the following example:

jugo de naranja

If you translated that example word for word, it would say *juice of orange*. But, of course, we would translate it into English as *orange juice*.

This usage of the word **de** is extremely common in Spanish, and you will see it many times in upcoming lessons.

LESSON 162

NEW WORDS **sopa / ensalada**

MEANING   *soup / salad*

Okay, breakfast is over. Time for lunch!

Both **sopa** and **ensalada** are feminine.

EXERCISES:

1. **A mí me encanta comer ensaladas.**
2. **Yo quiero almorzar sopa y ensalada.**
3. **Gracias por hacer una ensalada.**
4. **Mi gato está en la mesa y tiene hambre.**
5. **Yo quiero beber jugo de naranja con mi desayuno.**
6. **A mis niños les encantan las tostadas con mantequilla.**
7. **Más café, por favor.**
8. **Ella no puede ir al parque porque está almorzando con su familia ahora mismo.**
9. **Mis hijos desayunan todas las mañanas conmigo.**
10. **El señor Smith quiere almorzar sopa todos los días, pero a la señora Smith le gusta almorzar frutas y ensalada.**

Answers on page 263.

LESSON 163

NEW WORDS **pollo / pavo**

MEANING *chicken / turkey*

Pollo and **pavo** are both masculine.

EXERCISES:

1. **¿Quieres almorzar pollo?**
2. **Sí, yo quiero sopa de pollo.**
3. **Mi madre siempre cocina sopa de pollo.**
4. **El pavo está en la cocina en la mesa.**
5. **Mi mamá y mi papá están cocinando un pavo.**
6. **Nosotros nunca comemos cereal sin leche.**
7. **A mis padres les gusta desayunar tostadas y café todas las mañanas.**
8. **Yo no puedo beber leche, pero puedo beber jugo de naranja.**
9. **Nosotros siempre cargamos las frutas.**
10. **Las muchachas quieren ir a la biblioteca hoy porque necesitan más libros.**

Answers on page 264.

LESSON 164

NEW WORD **emparedado**

MEANING *sandwich*

Emparedado is masculine.

EXERCISES:

1. Yo almuerzo un emparedado todos los días.
2. Él quiere un emparedado de pavo.
3. ¿Quiere usted un emparedado de pollo?
4. Mi amigo está comiendo un emparedado, pero yo estoy bebiendo café.
5. A mi familia le encanta desayunar huevos, frutas y cereal con leche.
6. Nosotros almorzamos todos los días, pero nunca comemos emparedados.
7. Yo tengo sed y quiero beber jugo de naranja.
8. A mi madre no le gusta leche en su café.
9. Hay un emparedado de pollo en el comedor.
10. ¿A ti te gustan tus tostadas con mantequilla?

Answers on page 264.

LESSON 165

NEW WORDS **vegetal / papa**

MEANING *vegetable / potato*

PRONUNCIATION TIP: In the word **papa**, which means *potato*, the accent is on the first syllable, so it sounds like *PA-pa*. The word **papá**, on the other hand, which means *dad*, has the accent on the second syllable, so it sounds like *pa-PA*. Keep this in mind, as your father might be offended if you call him a *potato*.

Lunch is over. Please clean up after yourselves.

Vegetal is masculine, and **papa** is feminine.

EXERCISES:

1. **Mi madre está cocinando pollo, vegetales y papas para la cena.**
2. **A mi papá le encantan las papas.**
3. **Mamá, yo no quiero comer vegetales.**
4. **A mis niños no les gustan los vegetales.**
5. **A mí me gustan los emparedados de pavo.**
6. **El restaurante tiene sopas, ensaladas y emparedados.**
7. **Hoy nosotros estamos desayunando frutas.**
8. **Mi papá quiere almorzar un emparedado de pollo, pero yo quiero sopa de pollo.**
9. **¿A ti te gusta el jugo de naranja?**
10. **No, no me gusta el jugo de naranja, pero me encanta beber café.**

Answers on page 264.

LESSON 166

NEW WORDS **arroz / pan**

MEANING *rice / bread*

PRONUNCIATION TIP: In Spanish, the letter *z* always sounds like an *s* (except in Spain). So the word **arroz** will have a hissing **s** sound at the end, not a *z* sound.

If you are not on a low-carbohydrate diet (like the authors of this book should be), you might enjoy some **arroz** or some **pan** with your dinner.

Arroz and **pan** are both masculine.

EXERCISES:

1. **Más arroz y más ensalada, por favor.**
2. **Nosotros siempre cenamos pollo y arroz, pero almorzamos emparedados de pavo.**
3. **Nosotros no tenemos arroz pero tenemos pan.**
4. **Nosotros bebemos jugo de naranja todas las mañanas.**
5. **Tú puedes hacer un emparedado de pavo porque nosotras tenemos pan y pavo.**
6. **A mí me gustan las naranjas pero no me gustan los vegetales.**
7. **Nosotros no podemos hacer sopa de pollo porque no tenemos pollo.**
8. **Mi madre está haciendo una ensalada de fruta, pero a mí no me gustan las ensaladas.**
9. **Tú no puedes ir a la escuela sin tus libros.**
10. **El gato ve mi sopa, y tiene hambre.**

Answers on page 265.

LESSON 167

ADJECTIVES

An adjective is a word that describes a noun. For example:

> The <u>green</u> car
> The <u>hot</u> soup
> The <u>old</u> farmer

In Spanish, adjectives work together with nouns in a special way. An adjective must have the same number and gender as the noun it describes.

For instance, if a given noun is masculine, any adjective that goes with that noun must also be masculine. And if a given noun is plural, any adjective that goes with that noun must be plural, too.

Here is another thing you should be aware of: In English, the adjective usually comes first—before the noun it is describing. But in Spanish, the adjective usually comes *after* the noun. So in English, you might see a sentence like this:

> I have a <u>blue</u> car.

But in Spanish, that same sentence would be worded like this:

> I have a car <u>blue.</u>

In the next lesson, we will begin to learn some actual Spanish adjectives. With practice and repetition, you will quickly become accustomed to this word order.

LESSON 168

NEW WORD **nuevo**

MEANING *new*

In the last lesson, we learned that an adjective must have the same gender and number as the noun it describes. Now in this lesson, we will learn our first Spanish adjective, **nuevo**, which means *new*.

Let's use **nuevo** in some sentences to help us learn how Spanish adjectives work. Here's our first example:

El libro nuevo *(The new book)*

In that example, the adjective **nuevo** was describing the word **libro**. Since **libro** is masculine and singular, **nuevo** had to be masculine and singular too. Here's another example:

Las casas son nuevas *(The houses are new).*

In that example, **nuevas** was describing the word **casas**. Since **casas** was feminine and plural, **nuevas** had to be feminine and plural, too.

There will be four forms of **nuevo** in all, as seen in this handy chart:

	SINGULAR	PLURAL
MASCULINE	**nuevo**	**nuevos**
FEMININE	**nueva**	**nuevas**

Remember to use the **yo soy** verbs when talking about permanent things, and the **yo estoy** verbs when talking about temporary things.

EXERCISES:

1. **El libro es nuevo.**
2. **Mis padres tienen una casa nueva.**

3. **Me encanta el restaurante nuevo del Señor Smith.**
4. **A mí me gusta leer libros nuevos.**
5. **La sopa está en la cocina.**
6. **Nosotros necesitamos un perro nuevo.**
7. **Jennifer, Megan y Ashley son mis amigas nuevas.**
8. **Mi hermano quiere almorzar un emparedado de pavo y sopa.**
9. **Nosotros cenamos pollo, arroz y pan todas las noches.**
10. **Ustedes no pueden hacer una ensalada porque no tienen vegetales.**

Answers on page 265.

LESSON 169

NEW WORD **viejo**

MEANING *old*

There will be four forms of **viejo** in all, as seen in this handy chart:

	SINGULAR	PLURAL
MASCULINE	**viejo**	**viejos**
FEMININE	**vieja**	**viejas**

Now try these exercises.

EXERCISES:

1. **Yo no tengo hambre porque mi emparedado de pollo está viejo.**
2. **Las mujeres viejas son las amigas de mi madre.**
3. **La biblioteca no tiene libros viejos.**
4. **Mi padre quiere un trabajo nuevo.**
5. **Mi perro viejo está en el comedor.**
6. **A mi mamá no le gusta beber café viejo.**
7. **La biblioteca es vieja pero los libros son nuevos.**
8. **Las papas están viejas y también los vegetales.**
9. **A mis niños les encanta la sopa de pollo.**
10. **El perro quiere dormir en mi cama conmigo todas las noches.**

Answers on page 265.

LESSON 170

NEW WORD **muy**

MEANING *very*

EXERCISES:

1. **Mi emparedado está muy viejo.**
2. **Tu padre es muy viejo.**
3. **Mi ropa es muy vieja.**
4. **La escuela de mis hijas es nueva.**
5. **Nosotros tenemos un carro viejo pero necesitamos un carro nuevo.**
6. **A mis niños no les gusta leer libros viejos, pero les encantan los libros nuevos.**
7. **Yo quiero ir a un restaurante nuevo esta noche.**
8. **Nosotros comemos pan a menudo.**
9. **Nosotros no podemos dormir porque a nosotros no nos gusta la cama nueva.**
10. **Yo estoy haciendo cena para mis amigos.**

Answers on page 266.

LESSON 171

NEW WORDS **este, esta**

MEANING *this*

PRONUNCIATION TIP: Don't confuse the word **esta** with **está**. The word **esta**, one of our new words for this lesson, does not have an accent mark. When you pronounce it, you put the accent or stress on the first syllable, so it sounds like *ESS-ta*. But the word **está**, which means *he is, she is,* or *it is* has an accent mark over the final letter and sounds like *es-TAA*.

When studying any language it is very helpful to know how to say words such as *this* and *that*. In this lesson, let's learn how to say the word *this* by studying the Spanish words **este** and **esta**.

Este is masculine, so you would use it with masculine nouns, like this:

> **Este emparedado** *(this sandwich)*
> **Este hombre** *(this man)*

And **esta** is feminine, so you would use it with feminine nouns like this:

> **Esta ensalada** *(this salad)*
> **Esta mujer** *(this woman)*

To say the word *these*, we need to make **este** and **esta** plural. To make **esta** (the feminine form) plural, you would just add the letter *s*. But for **este** (the masculine form) the ending changes to **-os** leaving you with **estos**.

Here is a chart to help you study and remember these forms:

	SINGULAR	PLURAL
MASCULINE	**este**	**estos**
FEMININE	**esta**	**estas**

EXERCISES:

1. **Este carro es muy nuevo.**
2. **Estos huevos están muy viejos.**
3. **Esta ensalada está vieja.**
4. **Estas papas están muy viejas.**
5. **Yo quiero comprar este carro nuevo.**
6. **A mis hijos no les gustan estos vegetales.**
7. **Mi amigo quiere comer un emparedado.**
8. **Señor, a mí no me gusta esta ensalada.**
9. **A nosotros nos encantan los emparedados de pavo.**
10. **¿Bebes tú jugo de naranja todos los días?**

Answers on page 266.

LESSON 172

NEW WORDS   **ese, esa**

MEANING   *that*

In the last lesson we learned how to say *this* in Spanish. So now it's time to learn how to say *that*.

These forms are very similar to the words we studied in the last lesson. In fact, these forms are exactly like the forms from the last lesson but with the letter *t* removed.

To say the word *those*, we need to make **ese** and **esa** plural. To make **esa** (the feminine form) plural, you would just add the letter *s*. But for **ese** (the masculine form) the ending changes to **-os** leaving you with **esos**.

	SINGULAR	PLURAL
MASCULINE	**ese**	**esos**
FEMININE	**esa**	**esas**

EXERCISES:

1. **Ese carro es un carro nuevo.**
2. **Esos hombres son mis amigos.**
3. **Esa sopa está muy vieja.**
4. **Esas muchachas son mis hermanas.**
5. **¿Quieres tú comprar ese carro?**
6. **Gracias por hacer este emparedado.**
7. **Hay una papa vieja en la mesa.**
8. **Mi padre quiere comprar este carro.**
9. **A mis niños no les gusta dormir en esa cama.**
10. **Esa mujer tiene cinco niños.**

Answers on page 266.

LESSON 173

NEW WORD **hermoso**

MEANING *beautiful*

There will be four forms of **hermoso** in all, as seen in this handy chart:

	SINGULAR	PLURAL
MASCULINE	**hermoso**	**hermosos**
FEMININE	**hermosa**	**hermosas**

EXERCISES:

1. **Tu carro es hermoso.**
2. **Mi madre es muy hermosa.**
3. **Esos perros son hermosos.**
4. **La señora Smith es hermosa.**
5. **Estas muchachas son muy hermosas.**
6. **Esta ropa es la ropa nueva de mi hermana.**
7. **Él necesita comprar un carro nuevo.**
8. **Mis niños no pueden beber jugo de naranja.**
9. **Este gato está bebiendo leche.**
10. **Mi hermano está en esa casa.**

Answers on page 267.

LESSON 174

NEW WORDS **caliente / frío**

MEANING *hot / cold*

Caliente is different from the adjectives you have seen so far. It is the same for both genders, so there are really only two forms: the singular form, which is **caliente**, and the plural form, which is **calientes**.

Frío is a normal adjective with normal endings.

EXERCISES:

1. **Esta sopa está fría.**
2. **Esas papas están muy calientes.**
3. **Gracias por el agua fría.**
4. **Esta comida está caliente.**
5. **A mis niños les gusta la leche fría.**
6. **Ella quiere ir al centro comercial porque quiere comprar ropa nueva.**
7. **Al hombre viejo no le gusta cocinar.**
8. **Nosotros tenemos estas tres hijas hermosas.**
9. **El restaurante tiene emparedados fríos.**
10. **Mi huevo está frío.**

Answers on page 267.

LESSON 175

NEW WORDS   **grande / pequeño**

MEANING   *large* OR *big* / *small* OR *little*

Grande is similar to **caliente**. It also is an irregular adjective. **Grande** is the same for both genders, so there are only two forms of this adjective: the singular form, which is **grande**, and the plural form, which is **grandes**.

Pequeño is a normal adjective with normal endings.

EXERCISES:

1. **Tú tienes esa casa grande, pero nosotros tenemos esta casa pequeña.**
2. **Él tiene una casa grande y hermosa.**
3. **Mi perro tiene una cama pequeña, pero él quiere dormir en mi cama conmigo todas las noches.**
4. **Mi gato es muy pequeño y le gusta beber leche caliente.**
5. **Mi hermana no quiere este carro pequeño; ella quiere ese carro grande.**
6. **A mí no me gustan estos carros viejos.**
7. **El señor Jones está comprando una casa nueva hoy.**
8. **Esos huevos están muy calientes.**
9. **Yo como frutas todas las mañanas.**
10. **Yo veo a una mujer hermosa en el banco todas las semanas.**

Answers on page 267.

LESSON 176

NEW WORDS **caro / barato**

MEANING *expensive / cheap*

PRONUNCIATION TIP: You already know the word **carro**, which means *car*. But **caro**, one of the new words for this lesson, has only one *r*. These two words sound somewhat similar, but the word **carro** has a longer rolled *r* sound than **caro**.

EXERCISES:

1. **A mi hermano no le gusta la ropa barata.**
2. **Mi ropa es muy cara.**
3. **Ese restaurante tiene comida barata, pero la comida es vieja.**
4. **Mi padre tiene un carro caro.**
5. **Ellas siempre cargan esos libros grandes a la escuela.**
6. **Yo no puedo comer esta comida porque está muy fría.**
7. **Yo quiero una ensalada pequeña con mi cena.**
8. **¿Está la sopa caliente?**
9. **Mi madre es vieja y tiene un carro muy viejo.**
10. **¿Es este carro nuevo caro?**

Answers on page 268.

LESSON 177

NEW WORD **mucho**

MEANING *much, a lot of, many*

Mucho is a normal adjective with normal endings.

Mucho, unlike many other adjectives, goes <u>before</u> the noun it describes.

When **mucho** is singular, it means *much* or *a lot of*, as seen in the following examples:

> **mucho dinero** (*much money* OR *a lot of money*)
> **mucha comida** (*much food* OR *a lot of food*)

However, when **mucho** is plural, it means *many*, as seen in the following examples:

> **muchos carros** (*many cars*)
> **muchas casas** (*many houses*)

Also, the context of the sentence will help you to choose the correct translation for **mucho**.

EXERCISES:

1. **El señor Jones tiene mucho dinero.**
2. **Nosotros tenemos muchos libros.**
3. **Hoy nosotros estamos haciendo mucho trabajo.**
4. **Hay muchos emparedados en la cocina.**
5. **Mi perro bebe mucha agua todos los días.**
6. **Hay muchos niños en la escuela.**
7. **La biblioteca tiene muchos libros caros.**
8. **Mi madre está haciendo mucho pan.**
9. **Gracias por comprar este libro barato.**
10. **Adiós, amigos.**

Answers on page 268.

GENERAL ADVICE

Congratulations! You made it all the way to the end of the book!

In closing, the authors would like to offer a few thoughts which the reader may find helpful. This book was designed to cover the beginning stages of Spanish grammar in the easiest possible way. That means there is still a lot you do not know. So here are some suggestions to help you continue your study of Spanish.

First, we recommend that you take a closer look at the Spanish verb system. In this book, we have tried to help you build a good foundation of knowledge about Spanish verbs, but there is still much more to learn. For example, you still need to learn about the various Spanish verb tenses such as the perfect tense, future tense and other special Spanish verb tenses.

Also, in this book, in order to make memorization easier, we have only made use of a small number of words. So you should constantly strive to increase your Spanish vocabulary.

One way to do that is to use Spanish in real-life situations. Finding opportunities to speak Spanish in your daily life should not be too difficult because it is very likely that there are Spanish speakers in your area right now! Don't be afraid to try out your Spanish skills on some real Spanish speakers. By doing so, you will gain confidence and skill. You are bound to make mistakes, but mistakes are actually good—because when someone corrects you, you will learn from your mistakes.

Also, watching Spanish television shows can be very helpful, too. Whether you have cable television, satellite TV or just an old set of rabbit ears, you should be able to find a Spanish TV station to watch. You will be surprised how much you can learn just by watching TV.

One show in particular that I would like to mention is called *Destinos*. This show is an introductory Spanish course done in the format of a soap opera. Because the characters speak slowly, this show comes highly recommended for beginners. Look for it on your local PBS station.

Please take a moment to reflect on all you have learned. Although you have come a long way from lesson one, there is still much to learn. We, the authors, sincerely hope that this book has been enjoyable and profitable for you. We also hope that the knowledge you have gained from this book will become the foundation of a lifetime of enjoyment of the Spanish language.

ANSWER KEY

LESSON FOUR

1. *Boy*
2. *The boy*

LESSON SIX

1. *Girl*
2. *The girl*
3. *Boy*
4. *The boy*

LESSON SEVEN

1. *Boy and girl*
2. *Girl and boy*
3. *The boy and the girl*
4. *The girl and the boy*
5. *The boy*
6. *The girl*

LESSON EIGHT

1. *Boy*
2. *A boy*
3. *The boy*
4. *Boy and girl*
5. *The girl*
6. *The boy and the girl*
7. *The girl and the boy*

LESSON NINE

1. *Brother*
2. *A brother*
3. *The brother*
4. *Girl*
5. *The girl*
6. *Boy*
7. *The boy*
8. *A boy*
9. *The boy and the girl*
10. *The girl and the boy*

LESSON TEN

1. *A girl*
2. *A boy and a girl*
3. *A girl and a boy*
4. *A brother*
5. *The brother*
6. *The girl*
7. *The boy and the girl*
8. *A boy*
9. *The boy*
10. *The girl and the boy*

LESSON ELEVEN

1. *A sister*
2. *The sister*
3. *A brother and a sister*
4. *The sister and the brother*
5. *A boy*
6. *A girl*
7. *A boy and a girl*
8. *The brother and the sister*
9. *The girl*
10. *The girl and the boy*

LESSON TWELVE

1. *My sister*
2. *My brother*
3. *My brother and my sister*
4. *The brother*
5. *A brother and a sister*
6. *The sister*
7. *The girl*
8. *The boy and the girl*
9. *A sister*
10. *A girl*

LESSON 13

1. *Your sister*
2. *Your brother*
3. *My brother*
4. *Your brother and your sister*
5. *The boy*
6. *A girl and a boy*
7. *My sister*
8. *The sister and the brother*
9. *The girl*
10. *My sister and your sister*

LESSON 15

1. *The friend* (male)
2. *The friend* (female)
3. *A friend* (male)
4. *A friend* (female)
5. *Your friend* (female)
6. *My friend* (male)
7. *My friend* (female) *and your sister*
8. *My brother*
9. *The girl and the boy*
10. *My brother and your sister*

LESSON 16

1. *A young woman*
2. *A young man and a young woman*
3. *The young man*
4. *The young woman and the young man*
5. *My friend* (male)
6. *The friend* (female)
7. *Your friend* (female) *and your brother*
8. *The boy and the girl*
9. *Your sister*
10. *A boy*

LESSON 17

1. Plural
2. Singular
3. Singular
4. Singular
5. Plural
6. Singular
7. Plural
8. Plural
9. Plural
10. Singular

LESSON 18

1. **Muchachos**
2. **Niñas**
3. **Amigas**
4. **Niños**
5. **Muchachas**
6. **Hermanas**
7. **Amigos**
8. **Hermanos**

LESSON 20

1. *The young men*
2. *The sisters*
3. *The friends* (male or a group of mixed gender)
4. *The young women*
5. *The boys* OR *The children*
6. *Your sister and my brother*
7. *A friend* (female)
8. *The brothers* OR *The siblings*
9. *A friend* (male)
10. *The friend* (female)

LESSON 21

1. *A man*
2. *A woman*
3. *The man and the woman*
4. *The men and the women*
5. *My sister and my brother*
6. *Your friend* (male)
7. *The young women*
8. *The men*
9. *The girls*
10. *My friend* (female)

LESSON 22

1. *My brothers* OR *My siblings*
2. *Your friends* (female)
3. *My girls*
4. *Your friends* (male or a group of mixed gender)
5. *A man and a woman*
6. *The young women and the young men*
7. *My sister*
8. *My boys* OR *My children*
9. *The man and the woman*
10. *Your friend* (male)

LESSON 23

1. *My son*
2. *My daughters*
3. *Your sons* OR *your children*
4. *Your daughter and my son*
5. *A daughter and a son*
6. *My friend* (female)
7. *A man and a woman*
8. *The young women and the young men*
9. *My brother and your brothers* OR *My brother and your siblings*
10. *Your brother and my friends* (male or of mixed gender)

LESSON 24

1. *A man*
2. *Some men*
3. *A woman*
4. *Some women*
5. *The young women and the young men*
6. *My brother*
7. *Some boys* OR *Some children*
8. *Your friends* (male or of mixed gender)
9. *Some friends* (female)
10. *My daughters*

LESSON 25

1. *Hello, friend.*
2. *Goodbye, my friend.*
3. *Good morning, my friends.*
4. *Good afternoon, friends.*
5. *Good evening* OR *Good night.*
6. *Some young men and some young women.*
7. *My daughter and my son.*
8. *Your daughters.*
9. *The young women.*
10. *The man.*

LESSON 26

1. *Hello, Mom.*
2. *Good morning, Dad.*
3. *Your parents.*
4. *Good evening, Father* OR *Good night, Father.*
5. *My parents.*
6. *Good afternoon, my daughter.*
7. *A young man and a young woman.*
8. *Goodbye, my friends.*
9. *Good evening, Mom and Dad* OR *Good night, Mom and Dad.*
10. *Good morning, Mother.*

LESSON 27

1. Kate (subject) walks (verb)
2. car (subject) is (verb)
3. sister (subject) likes (verb)
4. horse (subject) is (verb)
5. Harry (subject) told (verb)
6. Jim (subject) played (verb)
7. Mark (subject) plays (verb)
8. sister (subject) cleans (verb)
9. Julia (subject) loves (verb)
10. students (subject) are doing (verb)

LESSON 28

1. he (takes the place of *Alfred)*
2. it (takes the place of *locker room)*
3. she
4. they (takes the place of *kids)*
5. he (takes the place of *Johnny)*
6. we
7. they
8. you
9. it (takes the place of *rabbit)*
10. they (takes the place of *children)*

LESSON 29

1. *I am your mother.*
2. *I am your sister.*
3. *I am a girl.*
4. *I am a young man.*
5. *Good morning, my friend.*
6. *Hello, Mom; hello, Dad.*
7. *I am a young woman.*
8. *I am a woman.*
9. *Goodbye, men.*
10. *Good evening, my friends* OR *Good night, my friends.*

LESSON 30

1. *I am not a girl.*
2. *I am not your father.*
3. *I am not your sister.*
4. *Goodbye, my friends.*
5. *Hello, Dad.*
6. *I am your friend.*
7. *Good afternoon, my brother.*
8. *I am not the man.*
9. *Good morning, Father.*
10. *Hello, young men and young women.*

LESSON 31

1. *You are my friend.*
2. *You are my mother.*
3. *You are not a girl.*
4. *You are the young man.*
5. *You are my father.*
6. *You are a woman.*
7. *I am not your sister.*
8. *Good evening, Mom* OR *Good night, Mom.*
9. *I am your brother.*
10. *You are my daughter.*

LESSON 33

1. *He is my father.*
2. *She is my mother.*
3. *My brother is a boy.*
4. *She is your sister.*
5. *She is my daughter.*
6. *I am your friend.*
7. *You are my dad.*
8. *I am not a mother.*
9. *You are not a woman.*
10. *I am a young woman.*

LESSON 34

1. *Good morning, sir.*
2. *Good morning, Mr. Jones.*
3. *Mr. Jones is my father.*
4. *He is my father.*
5. *Good morning, ma'am.*
6. *Good morning, Mrs. Johnson.*
7. *Mrs. Johnson is not my sister.*
8. *She is my sister.*
9. *Miss Smith is my daughter.*
10. *She is my daughter.*

LESSON 35

1. *We are friends.*
2. *We are your sisters.*
3. *We are not children.*
4. *Good morning, my sons* OR *Good morning, my children.*
5. *Goodbye, Mrs. Smith.*
6. *I am your mom.*
7. *You are my mother.*
8. *He is my friend.*
9. *She is a young woman.*
10. *I am your friend.*

LESSON 36

1. *Y'all are my friends.*
2. *Y'all are my sons* OR *Y'all are my children.*
3. *Y'all are sisters.*
4. *Good afternoon, my friend.*
5. *He is my dad.*
6. *Mr. Smith is my brother.*
7. *Goodbye, Mr. Smith.*
8. *We are not girls.*
9. *You are not my brother.*
10. *She is my friend.*

LESSON 38

1. *They are my brothers.*
2. *They are my friends.*
3. *They are my daughters.*
4. *Y'all are my friends.*
5. *We are men.*
6. *Good morning, Mr. Jones.*
7. *The women are my sisters.*
8. *She is my mom.*
9. *You are a young man.*
10. *We are friends.*

LESSON 40

1. *I* (subject) first person, singular
2. You (subject) second person, singular
3. She (subject) third person, singular
4. We (subject) first person, plural
5. Y'all (subject) second person, plural
6. They (subject) third person, plural
7. He (subject) third person, singular
8. It (subject) third person, singular
9. Y'all (subject) second person, plural
10. flowers (subject) third person, plural

LESSON 42

1. *One man* OR *A man.*
2. *One sister* OR *A sister.*
3. *552-4106 (five five two four one zero six).*
4. *Two women.*
5. *Three sons* OR *Three children.*
6. *Five women.*
7. *Six men and four women.*
8. *They are my brothers* OR *They are my siblings.*
9. *We are your parents.*
10. *He is my father.*

LESSON 43

1. *Seven young women.*
2. *Eight children*
3. *898-0417 (eight nine eight zero four one seven).*
4. *Ten parents.*
5. *Eleven friends.*
6. *Twelve sons* OR *Twelve children.*
7. *You are my friend.*
8. *Miss Smith is not my sister.*
9. *My mother is Mrs. Jones.*
10. *They are my friends.*

LESSON 44

1. *Five cats.*
2. *Four dogs.*
3. *Three brothers and two sisters.*
4. *Six cats and nine dogs.*
5. *Seven friends.*
6. *My dogs and my (female) cat.*
7. *Eleven children.*
8. *They are my daughters.*
9. *I am your friend.*
10. *Hello, my children.*

LESSON 45

1. *I have a cat* OR *I have one cat.*
2. *I have two (female) dogs.*
3. *I have ten cats and a dog* OR *I have ten cats and one dog.*
4. *I have some cats.*
5. *You are my daughter.*
6. *Your sister is my sister.*
7. *I have a son.*
8. *She is my sister.*
9. *I have the dogs.*
10. *Mr. Smith is my friend.*

LESSON 46

1. *I have eight dogs and also a cat.*
2. *I have four brothers and also three sisters.*
3. *I have twelve cats.*
4. *I do not have a daughter.*
5. *Good morning, Miss.*
6. *My dog is my friend.*
7. *Hello, Mrs. Smith.*
8. *Mrs. Jones is my mom.*
9. *I have some dogs and some cats also.*
10. *I am a woman.*

LESSON 47

1. *I have money.*
2. *I do not have money.*
3. *I do not have your money.*
4. *They are my sisters.*
5. *We are friends.*
6. *I have some cats and also a dog.*
7. *Good evening, sir* OR *Good night, sir.*
8. *I have three children.*
9. *Your sister is my friend.*
10. *Goodbye, Miss Smith.*

LESSON 48

1. *I have a dollar.*
2. *I have ten dollars.*
3. *I have four dollars.*
4. *I have money.*
5. *I have seven cats and also a dog.*
6. *Good afternoon, Miss.*
7. *The girls are my daughters.*
8. *My parents are Mr. Smith and Mrs. Smith.*
9. *She is my daughter.*
10. *Mrs. Jones is my friend.*

LESSON 49

1. *You have my money.*
2. *You have nine dogs and also a cat.*
3. *You have my dog.*
4. *I do not have your money.*
5. *I am not a father.*
6. *My dog is my friend.*
7. *You have eight dollars.*
8. *Mr. Smith is my father.*
9. *Goodbye, Mother.*
10. *We are not brothers* OR *We are not siblings.*

LESSON 50

1. *He has a dog.*
2. *She has a cat.*
3. *He does not have money.*
4. *She has six dollars.*
5. *He has four children.*
6. *Goodbye, my friends.*
7. *You have two sisters and also a brother.*
8. *I have seven dollars.*
9. *They are my friends.*
10. *We are not children.*

LESSON 51

1. *I do not have a sister, but you have three sisters.*
2. *He does not have money, but she has eleven dollars.*
3. *You do not have a cat, but she has seven cats.*
4. *My cat is my friend.*
5. *Mr. Jones is my father and Mrs. Jones is my mother.*
6. *We are friends.*
7. *Good morning, Miss.*
8. *I have four dogs and also a cat.*
9. *The young women are my friends.*
10. *I have some friends.*

LESSON 52

1. *We have friends.*
2. *We do not have money, but you have five dollars.*
3. *We have two sisters.*
4. *You have a dollar OR You have one dollar.*
5. *Mrs. Smith is my mother.*
6. *She has five sons and two daughters.*
7. *The girls are my sisters.*
8. *You have eight dollars.*
9. *You are my friend, but he is my brother.*
10. *She has a brother and also a sister.*

LESSON 53

1. *Y'all have three dogs.*
2. *Y'all do not have money.*
3. *Y'all do not have money, but we have nine dollars.*
4. *Y'all have six dollars.*
5. *The man has a cat and a dog.*
6. *He is not my friend.*
7. *They are my friends.*
8. *The man does not have a cat, but the woman has four cats.*
9. *The children are your brothers and your sisters.*
10. *You have seven sisters.*

LESSON 54

1. *They have twelve dollars.*
2. *They have three sisters.*
3. *They have two children, but we do not have children.*
4. *You do not have a brother, but I have two sisters.*
5. *I have four cats and also some dogs.*
6. *You are my friend.*
7. *My parents are my friends.*
8. *Good evening, my friends* OR *Good night, my friends.*
9. *The young men are my sons.*
10. *Mr. Smith has three sons* OR *Mr. Smith has three children.*

LESSON 57

rex becomes **rey**
exercitus becomes **ejército**
homo becomes **hombre**
terra becomes **tierra**
veritas becomes **verdad**
octo becomes **ocho**
arbor becomes **árbol**
stella becomes **estrella**

LESSON 58

1. *The mother has her child.*
2. *My brother has his money.*
3. *My friend has his dogs, but I do not have my dog.*
4. *We have four brothers* OR *We have four siblings.*
5. *The children have a cat.*
6. *You are my friend.*
7. *She has seven dollars.*
8. *My parents have eleven sons* OR *My parents have eleven children.*
9. *I have some dogs and also a cat.*
10. *Goodbye, Dad.*

LESSON 60

1. *The woman's friend.*
2. *My mother's sister.*
3. *My sister's dog.*
4. *My parents' money.*
5. *They have three dollars, but I do not have money.*
6. *My children have five dollars.*
7. *The young men have money.*
8. *My friend has four dogs.*
9. *I am a girl.*
10. *The man has his money.*

LESSON 61

1. *The man's children.*
2. *The young man's sister.*
3. *The boy's friends.*
4. *I do not have the young man's money.*
5. *We do not have the woman's dog.*
6. *They have six children, two cats and a dog.*
7. *My mother has ten dollars, but my father does not have his money.*
8. *She has her parents' money.*
9. *We do not have a cat.*
10. *We are your parents.*

LESSON 62

1. *My sister's car.*
2. *I have my Dad's car.*
3. *The man's money.*
4. *My friend's car.*
5. *The man's cat.*
6. *My brother has his car.*
7. *You do not have a car.*
8. *We have eight dollars, but you do not have money.*
9. *Good evening, Mr. Jones* OR *Good night, Mr. Jones.*
10. *She has her mother's car and also her money.*

LESSON 63

1. *I have a dog.*
2. *I have a dog.*
3. *You have a cat.*
4. *You have a cat.*
5. *He does not have a brother, but he has two sisters.*
6. *We are friends.*
7. *We are friends.*
8. *I am a man.*
9. *My father does not have his car, but he has his money.*
10. *They have my mom's cat.*

LESSON 65

1. *I am hungry.*
2. *I am hungry.*
3. *I am thirsty.*
4. *I am thirsty.*
5. *My dog is hungry.*
6. *They are thirsty.*
7. *You do not have a car.*
8. *We do not have a cat, but we have a dog.*
9. *My son has the man's car.*
10. *Your friend has his dog.*

LESSON 66

1. *Dad, I want a cat.*
2. *He wants ten dollars.*
3. *We want a car.*
4. *You want five dollars.*
5. *They want my brother's dog.*
6. *My sister has a dog.*
7. *My dog is hungry.*
8. *I am thirsty, but you are not thirsty.*
9. *My sister has twelve dollars.*
10. *They want my dad's money.*

LESSON 70

1. *They want food.*
2. *We are hungry, but we do not have food.*
3. *My dad wants food.*
4. *The cats are hungry.*
5. *They are hungry, but they do not have money.*
6. *They want a cat and some dogs.*
7. *We have the car.*
8. *The dog wants the cat's food.*
9. *My children want my money.*
10. *Mrs. Jones wants money also.*

LESSON 71

1. *You want food because you are hungry.*
2. *I do not have a car because I do not have money.*
3. *We are hungry, but we do not have food.*
4. *My friend wants a dog.*
5. *My father does not have his dog.*
6. *My friends are thirsty.*
7. *The children have seven dollars.*
8. *I have a dog.*
9. *We want food because we are hungry.*
10. *Goodbye, my friends.*

LESSON 72

1. *I want water because I am thirsty.*
2. *They want water because they are thirsty.*
3. *My cat is hungry and he wants food.*
4. *Good afternoon, Mr. Smith.*
5. *We are hungry, but we do not have money.*
6. *I have two cats.*
7. *Mr. Jones has a daughter and also three sons.*
8. *The men are hungry, but the women are not hungry.*
9. *My sister wants my dad's car.*
10. *You are my friend.*

LESSON 74

1. *I speak English.*
2. *You speak Spanish.*
3. *My parents speak English.*
4. *We speak Spanish and also English.*
5. *The dog is hungry.*
6. *She wants food and water.*
7. *The children are hungry and thirsty.*
8. *The woman's cat is hungry.*
9. *She does not speak Spanish.*
10. *We are thirsty because we do not have water.*

LESSON 75

1. *I always speak Spanish.*
2. *My children always want my car and my money.*
3. *They always want my car.*
4. *You are always hungry.*
5. *My friends always speak Spanish.*
6. *I am hungry because I do not have food.*
7. *We do not always speak English.*
8. *She has seven cats.*
9. *They do not want a dog.*
10. *Your children want water.*

LESSON 76

1. *I speak English every day.*
2. *My cat wants my food every day.*
3. *Every day you speak Spanish.*
4. *She has a dog and four cats.*
5. *We have ten dollars.*
6. *We want water because we are thirsty.*
7. *My dog always wants food.*
8. *They speak Spanish every day, but we speak English.*
9. *My Dad's friends are hungry.*
10. *You are my sister but also you are my friend.*

LESSON 77

1. *Every day I buy food.*
2. *We buy food every day.*
3. *The women buy food every day.*
4. *My sister's cat is hungry.*
5. *I do not have food and I do not have money.*
6. *You want water because you are thirsty.*
7. *We speak Spanish every day.*
8. *My sister does not speak English, but she speaks Spanish.*
9. *Good morning, children.*
10. *You always speak English, but I always speak Spanish.*

LESSON 78

1. *You have a dog.*
2. *Do you have a dog?*
3. *They buy food every day.*
4. *Do they buy food every day?*
5. *We have six cats.*
6. *Do we have six cats?*
7. *He speaks Spanish.*
8. *Does he speak Spanish?*
9. *I want my Dad's car.*
10. *My daughter does not have her car.*

LESSON 79

1. *Do you buy food every day?*
2. *No, I do not buy food every day.*
3. *Does your brother have a child?*
4. *Yes, my brother has three sons and also a daughter.*
5. *Are the men hungry?*
6. *Yes, the men are always hungry.*
7. *Are you a mother?*
8. *No, I am not a mother because I do not have children.*
9. *Do you speak Spanish?*
10. *No, I speak English, but my sisters speak Spanish every day.*

LESSON 80

1. *I eat food every day.*
2. *The young men eat food every day.*
3. *We eat every day.*
4. *Is Miss Smith hungry?*
5. *No, Miss Smith is not hungry, but I am hungry.*
6. *They buy food every day.*
7. *My sister's children have five dogs.*
8. *Good afternoon, children.*
9. *I have nine children.*
10. *We always speak Spanish.*

LESSON 81

1. *Every day I drink water.*
2. *She is thirsty but she does not want water.*
3. *My brothers speak Spanish every day.*
4. *Do you drink water every day?*
5. *Yes, I drink water every day.*
6. *My Dad has a dog and also two cats.*
7. *We eat food and drink water every day.*
8. *He eats food because he is hungry.*
9. *My parents buy food every day.*
10. *They are my friends.*

LESSON 82

1. *We buy food every week.*
2. *Every week they buy food.*
3. *Your parents buy food every week.*
4. *My mother's dog is always hungry.*
5. *We want food and money.*
6. *My cats want my food every day.*
7. *The young woman speaks English and Spanish also.*
8. *The men are my brothers.*
9. *Does your son want a car?*
10. *Yes, my son always wants his father's car.*

LESSON 83

1. *I work every day.*
2. *My sisters work every day.*
3. *We buy food every week.*
4. *Do you work every day?*
5. *Yes, I work every day.*
6. *They are my sisters.*
7. *They do not speak English, but they speak Spanish.*
8. *We are thirsty because we do not have water.*
9. *My children always have money because they work every day.*
10. *My dogs eat food every day, and they always drink water.*

LESSON 84

1. *I eat with my sisters every week.*
2. *He works with my brother every day.*
3. *I speak English with my friends, but I speak Spanish with my parents.*
4. *I drink water every day.*
5. *We speak Spanish every day.*
6. *My children do not speak English, but they speak Spanish.*
7. *I have some friends.*
8. *My friends are hungry and thirsty.*
9. *Do we have food?*
10. *No, we do not have food, but we have water.*

LESSON 85

1. *She eats with me every week.*
2. *They eat with you every week.*
3. *Do they eat with you every day?*
4. *Yes, they eat with me every day.*
5. *The young women want water because they are thirsty.*
6. *Your dog wants water.*
7. *My brother works with me every day.*
8. *My brother speaks Spanish, but I speak English.*
9. *Mr. Smith works every day.*
10. *My dogs always drink water.*

LESSON 86

1. *I go with you every week.*
2. *You go with me every day.*
3. *We go every week, but they go every day.*
4. *Do you go every week?*
5. *They go with me every day.*
6. *He goes with my friends every week.*
7. *Do the men work every day?*
8. *Yes, the men work every day.*
9. *We drink water every day.*
10. *Good morning, Mrs. Williams.*

LESSON 87

1. *I go to the store every week.*
2. *My mother goes to the bank every week.*
3. *Do your parents go to the store every day?*
4. *No, they go to the store every week.*
5. *She goes to the bank every week.*
6. *I go to my father's store every day.*
7. *She eats with me every day.*
8. *You go to the store with me every week.*
9. *The young men and the young women work every day.*
10. *My dogs are always hungry.*

LESSON 88

1. *I see the car.*
2. *We see your dog every day.*
3. *Do you see the money?*
4. *No, I do not see the money.*
5. *We go to the store every week.*
6. *You work with my father every day.*
7. *She drinks water every day.*
8. *Good afternoon, Miss Jones.*
9. *My sister eats with me every day.*
10. *They always speak Spanish.*

LESSON 89

1. *I see my friends every day.*
2. *Do you see your friends every day?*
3. *She sees her father every week.*
4. *We see the children every day.*
5. *My son buys food every week.*
6. *Do you want a dog?*
7. *Yes, I want a dog and also a cat.*
8. *You go to the bank with your father every week.*
9. *My dog does not work, but he always eats.*
10. *My children want a cat.*

LESSON 90

1. *Do you have a car?*
2. *Do you have a car?*
3. *Do we have four dogs?*
4. *Do we have four dogs?*
5. *Do you see Mr. Smith every day?*
6. *Do you see Mr. Smith every day?*
7. *Do you go to the store every week?*
8. *Do you go to the store every week?*
9. *I go to the store with you every week.*
10. *My sister wants my parents' car.*

LESSON 91

1. *We go to the mall every week.*
2. *I go to the mall with my friends every day.*
3. *My daughters go to the mall every day.*
4. *Do you go to the bank every week?*
5. *Yes, I go to the bank every week.*
6. *They see my dad every day.*
7. *My children want a cat.*
8. *You go with me to the mall every week because we are friends.*
9. *Does your mother speak Spanish?*
10. *No, my mother does not speak Spanish.*

LESSON 92

1. *I go to the bank often.*
2. *You do not go to the store often, but I go to the store every week.*
3. *Do you speak English often?*
4. *Yes, I always speak English, but my friends speak Spanish.*
5. *Do you see your sisters often?*
6. *Yes, I see my sisters every week.*
7. *We drink water often because we are always thirsty.*
8. *We see my brother's children every week.*
9. *I go with you to the mall every week.*
10. *The women work every day.*

LESSON 93

1. *I never go to the mall, but my parents go every week.*
2. *Do you go to the store often?*
3. *No, I never go to the store.*
4. *We go to the mall often, but we never have money.*
5. *Do you buy food often?*
6. *Yes, I go to the store every day.*
7. *My dog drinks water often because he is thirsty.*
8. *My father's friends work every day.*
9. *I do not want a dog, because dogs are always hungry.*
10. *I see my friends every day.*

LESSON 94

1. *I never go to the mall without money.*
2. *My mom never goes to the bank without money.*
3. *I never go to the mall without my friends.*
4. *The women speak Spanish every day.*
5. *Does he go to the mall often?*
6. *Yes, he goes to the mall every week.*
7. *My brother and his friends always go to the mall.*
8. *My father's sister never goes to the store without money.*
9. *We go to the mall with my parents every week.*
10. *I see my friends every day.*

LESSON 95

1. *I never go to the park.*
2. *They go to the park every week.*
3. *Do you go to the park with your friends often?*
4. *Yes, I always go to the park with my friends.*
5. *You are my friend.*
6. *We always speak Spanish, but my parents never speak Spanish.*
7. *Do you go to the store often?*
8. *Yes, I go to the store with you every week.*
9. *We never go to the mall without money.*
10. *My Dad's dog is always hungry.*

LESSON 96

1. *My friends go to the beach often.*
2. *Do you go to the beach often?*
3. *No, I never go to the beach.*
4. *He goes to the beach with his parents every week.*
5. *They always go to the beach, but we always go to the park.*
6. *You never go to the mall without money.*
7. *We are friends.*
8. *I want my sister's car.*
9. *They see Mrs. Jones every week.*
10. *He never goes to the store with you.*

LESSON 97

1. *has*
2. *is*
3. *goes*
4. *Has*
5. *prefers*

LESSON 98

1. *You are.*
2. *You are Mr. Johnson.*
3. *Are you Mr. Johnson?*
4. *You have a cat.*
5. *Do you have a cat?*
6. *You speak English.*
7. *Do you speak Spanish?*
8. *Do you go to the beach often?*
9. *You never go to the bank.*
10. *Do you have some children?*

LESSON 99

1. *Y'all are my friends.*
2. *Do y'all have a cat?*
3. *Y'all go to the beach every week.*
4. *Do y'all go to the mall often?*
5. *Y'all never go to the mall without money.*
6. *Are you Mr. Smith?*
7. *Do y'all speak English?*
8. *We never go to the park without food and without water.*
9. *My parents go to the mall with me often.*
10. *I speak Spanish with you, but I speak English with my parents.*

LESSON 100

1. *I go to my job every day.*
2. *I want a job.*
3. *My father goes to his job every day.*
4. *My friend wants a job because he wants a car.*
5. *I work every day.*
6. *Mrs. Jones never goes to the mall without her money.*
7. *Do y'all go to the park every week?*
8. *No, we never go to the park, but we go to the beach often.*
9. *My sister has some dogs and also a cat.*
10. *Are you Miss Smith?*

LESSON 101

1. *Your family goes to the store every week.*
2. *My brother goes to the beach with his family every week.*
3. *My family eats with me every day.*
4. *The woman and the children are my family.*
5. *I have a job and a car.*
6. *You are Mr. Williams.*
7. *Y'all are my friends.*
8. *Are you Mrs. Jones?*
9. *Do you go to the park every week?*
10. *She goes to her job every day.*

LESSON 102

1. *Do you go to the beach with your sister every week?*
2. *The man goes to his job every day.*
3. *You go to the bank with your children every week.*
4. *Do you go to the mall with your friends every week?*
5. *We drink water every day.*
6. *Do you have your dog?*
7. *Do you go to the park with your family often?*
8. *Do y'all speak Spanish?*
9. *Do you speak Spanish with your friends?*
10. *I want water because I am thirsty.*

LESSON 103

1. *My family walks to the park every day.*
2. *Do you walk to the beach every week?*
3. *My friends walk to the beach every week.*
4. *I walk to the store with my mom every week.*
5. *I walk to the park with you often.*
6. *She never walks to the beach with me.*
7. *We walk to the beach often, but we never go to the park.*
8. *He walks to the beach with his friends every week.*
9. *Do y'all walk to the park often?*
10. *I do not have a car because I do not have a job.*

LESSON 104

1. to wash
2. to play
3. There is no infinitive in this sentence.
4. to be
5. to forgive
6. to return
7. to play
8. There is no infinitive in this sentence.
9. to buy
10. There is no infinitive in this sentence.

LESSON 105

1. *I want to buy a car.*
2. *They want to buy food.*
3. *We do not want to buy a cat.*
4. *He goes to the store every week because he wants to buy food.*
5. *She wants to buy her brother's car.*
6. *My family never walks to the beach without water.*
7. *Sir, is Mrs. Jones your sister?*
8. *Y'all are my brothers and sisters.*
9. *Hello, sir—are you Mr. Smith?*
10. *Yes, I am Mr. Smith.*

LESSON 107

1. **hablo, hablas, habla, hablamos, habláis, hablan**
2. **trabajo, trabajas, trabaja, trabajamos, trabajáis, trabajan**
3. **como, comes, come, comemos, coméis, comen**
4. **camino, caminas, camina, caminamos, camináis, caminan**

LESSON 108

1. *I want to buy clothes.*
2. *Dad, do you want to buy clothes?*
3. *We do not want to walk to the store.*
4. *We want to have a cat.*
5. *Are y'all hungry?*
6. *Do you have a job?*
7. *Mr. Jones' family goes to the beach often.*
8. *He wants to go to the store.*
9. *My cat never works, but he is always hungry.*
10. *I want to drink water because I am thirsty.*

LESSON 109

1. *I want to go to the beach today.*
2. *We do not want to go to the bank today.*
3. *You want to walk to the beach every day.*
4. *My friends want to go to the mall.*
5. *They want to buy clothes.*
6. *Do you go to the mall with your family often?*
7. *No, we never go to the mall.*
8. *We are Mrs. Jones' children.*
9. *She never goes to the park without her dog.*
10. *I want to have a cat, but I do not want a dog.*

LESSON 110

1. *I need to drink water because I am thirsty.*
2. *My dad needs to buy food.*
3. *They need to go to the store because they need to buy clothes.*
4. *We want to go to the beach today.*
5. *Do you have a family, Mr. Williams?*
6. *My parents want to have a dog.*
7. *My parents' dog is always hungry.*
8. *The young woman wants to go to the mall with her friends.*
9. *Do you walk to the beach often?*
10. *Yes, I go to the beach every day.*

LESSON 111

1. *I need to go to the bank tomorrow.*
2. *We want to go to the beach tomorrow.*
3. *She needs to go to the store today, but tomorrow she wants to go to the bank.*
4. *I need to go to the mall because I want to buy clothes.*
5. *Do y'all walk to the beach often?*
6. *Do y'all want to go to the park?*
7. *Do you want to go to the mall with me?*
8. *No, I never go to the mall.*
9. *We want to speak Spanish.*
10. *I am hungry.*

LESSON 112

1. *I am able to (I can) walk to the park.*
2. *I am able to (I can) speak Spanish.*
3. *I am able to (I can) go to the park tomorrow.*
4. *I am not able to (I cannot) buy a car.*
5. *I am able to (I can) work.*
6. *We want to buy clothes today.*
7. *She does not need to buy clothes, but she wants to go to the mall.*
8. *My cats are my friends.*
9. *Do you have some children?*
10. *We never go to the beach.*

LESSON 113

1. *You are not able to (you cannot) walk to the bank.*
2. *She is able to (she can) buy a car.*
3. *We are able to (we can) go to the park, but we are not able to (we cannot) go to the beach.*
4. *Are you able to (can you) go with me to the store?*
5. *They are not able to (they cannot) have a cat.*
6. *We need a dog.*
7. *I am not able to (I cannot) go to the mall tomorrow, but I am able to (I can) go today.*
8. *Do y'all want to go to the mall?*
9. *Y'all see Mrs. Jones every week.*
10. *We do not go to the store without money.*

LESSON 114

1. *We walk to school every day.*
2. *I do not want to go to school today!*
3. *I walk to school with my friends every day.*
4. *The young men do not want to work today.*
5. *My dog wants to go to school with me.*
6. *Do you want to walk with me to school?*
7. *I do not want to go to the store today because I do not need food.*
8. *You are not able to (you cannot) go to the store without money.*
9. *Do y'all need water?*
10. *She wants to go to the mall tomorrow because she wants to buy clothes.*

LESSON 115

1. *I have ten books.*
2. *I want to buy some books.*
3. *My sisters want to buy some books, but they are not able (they cannot) because they have no money.*
4. *My dogs walk to school with me every day.*
5. *My cat is hungry.*
6. *I need my books today because I need to go to school.*
7. *You have my sister's book.*
8. *We do not want to go to school tomorrow.*
9. *He wants to see his friends.*
10. *Do you go to the park often?*

LESSON 116

1. *I carry my books to school every day.*
2. *We always carry food and water to the park.*
3. *My parents always carry money.*
4. *I walk with my dogs every day.*
5. *He is not able to (he cannot) carry my brother.*
6. *We need some books.*
7. *She does not want to walk to the beach tomorrow.*
8. *Do y'all carry food and water?*
9. *No, but we are hungry and thirsty.*
10. *I want to drink water.*

LESSON 117

1. *I read a book every week.*
2. *Do you want to read a book?*
3. *We do not want to read a book today.*
4. *My children want to read books, but they do not want to work.*
5. *You are able to (you can) read a book.*
6. *Do y'all want to go to school?*
7. *You need to go to school tomorrow.*
8. *We carry books every day.*
9. *Do you have my brother's book?*
10. *They are able to (they can) read.*

LESSON 118

1. *I want to read the newspaper.*
2. *My parents read the newspaper every day.*
3. *I have a job; I carry the newspapers every day.*
4. *My mother reads the newspaper with my father every day.*
5. *My brother is not able to (he cannot) read the newspaper.*
6. *I want my father's newspaper.*
7. *Do you go to the beach with your family every week?*
8. *Yes, my family always goes with me to the beach.*
9. *They are not able to (they cannot) carry the books today.*
10. *I do not want to go to school tomorrow.*

LESSON 119

1. *She goes to church every week.*
2. *My children go to church with me every week.*
3. *Do y'all go to church every week?*
4. *Yes, we always go to church.*
5. *We are not able to (we cannot) walk to church.*
6. *Y'all carry the books to school every day.*
7. *I am not able to (I cannot) read the book.*
8. *My brother wants water because he is thirsty.*
9. *Mr. Jones never goes to church.*
10. *Do you want the newspaper today?*

LESSON 120

1. *I want to read books but I am not able to (I cannot) go to the library.*
2. *My friends go to the library every week.*
3. *Do you want to go to the library?*
4. *Do you want to go to the library?*
5. *No, I do not want to read books today, but I am able to (I can) go to the library with you tomorrow.*
6. *I want some books from the library.*
7. *We never go to church, but we need to go every week.*
8. *My dogs are not able to (they cannot) read the newspaper.*
9. *He always carries a newspaper.*
10. *The dog has my dad's newspaper.*

LESSON 122

1. *My parents often go to the mall to buy clothes.*
2. *He never goes to the library to read books and newspapers.*
3. *My daughter goes to the library to read books every day.*
4. *I go to the mall every week to see my friends.*
5. *You go to the store every day to work.*
6. *She always goes to the park to walk.*
7. *We go to church every week.*
8. *Y'all are not able to (y'all cannot) buy a car.*
9. *Every day I walk to the library to read books.*
10. *They need to go to the mall to buy clothes.*

LESSON 123

1. *We go to the restaurant every week.*
2. *I go to the restaurant often to eat with my friends.*
3. *My family goes to the restaurant to eat every week.*
4. *Do you want to go to the restaurant to eat?*
5. *Yes, I want to eat because I am hungry!*
6. *We are not able to (we cannot) go to the restaurant today because we do not have money.*
7. *He does not have his newspaper, but he has his books.*
8. *I never go to church, but I go to my job every day.*
9. *Do you read a book every week?*
10. *Yes, I read two books every week.*

LESSON 124

1. *They go to the restaurant to eat every night.*
2. *I want to go to the restaurant tonight.*
3. *The women want to go to church tonight.*
4. *Do you want to go to the library with me tonight?*
5. *Mr. Smith always carries the newspaper to the park.*
6. *Are we able to (can we) go to the mall to buy clothes tonight?*
7. *No, but you are able to (you can) go to the library to read your book.*
8. *We do not want to go to church tonight.*
9. *We want to walk to the park every night.*
10. *He never goes to school without his books.*

LESSON 125

1. *I have breakfast every day.*
2. *My family has breakfast every day.*
3. *I want to have breakfast, but we do not have food.*
4. *Do you want to have breakfast with me today?*
5. *Your parents go to the restaurant to eat every night.*
6. *He wants to go to a restaurant to have breakfast.*
7. *He wants to go to a restaurant to have breakfast.*
8. *I want to buy a car but I do not have money.*
9. *Y'all want to have breakfast because y'all are hungry.*
10. *I carry food with me every day.*

LESSON 126

1. *I do not want to work this morning.*
2. *My family has breakfast with me every morning.*
3. *My sister goes to school every morning.*
4. *We have breakfast every morning.*
5. *I want to have breakfast with my family this morning.*
6. *My father reads the newspaper every morning.*
7. *They want to go to the restaurant every morning to have breakfast.*
8. *Do you go to the beach often with your family?*
9. *No, we never go to the beach, but we go to the park often.*
10. *I drink water every morning.*

LESSON 127

1. *My friends have lunch with me every day.*
2. *Do you want to have lunch with me?*
3. *Yes, I want to have lunch with you.*
4. *Fred Smith, my friend, wants to have lunch with me today.*
5. *We need to have lunch.*
6. *She has breakfast with her parents every morning.*
7. *I want to go to the restaurant with you.*
8. *I have lunch with my friends every day.*
9. *They want to have lunch with Michael every day.*
10. *Y'all never read the newspaper.*

LESSON 128

1. *I want to go to the beach now.*
2. *I want to have lunch right now because I am hungry!*
3. *My dogs want to eat right now.*
4. *She wants to read her newspaper now.*
5. *I want to go to the mall now to buy clothes.*
6. *Are you able to (can you) go to the mall with me?*
7. *We read books every day.*
8. *Do you have ten dollars?*
9. *Yes, but I want to go to the store to buy food.*
10. *The young women go to the restaurant every night to eat.*

LESSON 129

1. *I have dinner with my family every night.*
2. *They go to the restaurant to have dinner every night.*
3. *I do not want to have lunch; I want to have dinner.*
4. *My sister has dinner with me every week.*
5. *We have breakfast every morning.*
6. *She wants to have dinner with her friends every night.*
7. *I want to have dinner right now because I am hungry.*
8. *Do you want to go to the library to read books?*
9. *No, I want to go to the beach.*
10. *You are not able to (you cannot) go to the store because you do not have a car.*

LESSON 132

1. *I work at a bank.*
2. *My sister is in the car.*
3. *We are at the library.*
4. *I want to be at the beach.*
5. *They are at the park.*
6. *You are in a church.*
7. *I am in the restaurant to have lunch.*
8. *Your cats want to eat right now.*
9. *We need to buy food tonight.*
10. *I need to have dinner now.*

LESSON 133

1. *My father's newspaper is on the desk.*
2. *The cats are on the table!*
3. *The food is not on the table, but we want to have dinner.*
4. *Your friends are at the beach, but you are at the library.*
5. *My family is at the park now.*
6. *We are at a restaurant because we want to have lunch.*
7. *Do you have a dog?*
8. *No, but I have some cats.*
9. *Y'all are my friends.*
10. *He is my father.*

LESSON 134

1. *My children are in the house now.*
2. *My cat is not in the house.*
3. *The cats are in the house.*
4. *The cat is on the table and he wants my food.*
5. *I carry my books often because I want to read.*
6. *My mom is hungry and she wants to have dinner right now.*
7. *The young men go to the restaurant to eat every night.*
8. *We are at the beach.*
9. *My father wants to read the newspaper, but the newspaper is not on the desk.*
10. *Do you want to have dinner at a restaurant?*

LESSON 135

1. *The food is in the kitchen.*
2. *The table is in the dining room.*
3. *The newspaper is in the living room.*
4. *The children are in the living room.*
5. *Without a table, we are not able to (we cannot) have dinner.*
6. *I am in the house.*
7. *You are always at the library, but you never read the books.*
8. *My dad wants his newspaper, but it is not on his desk.*
9. *My family has breakfast every morning.*
10. *My mother is in the dining room, but she does not want to have dinner because she is not hungry.*

LESSON 136

1. *My sister is in her bedroom.*
2. *The cats are on my bed.*
3. *Are the children in the bed?*
4. *The dogs are in the bed with my parents.*
5. *My bed and my desk are in my bedroom.*
6. *My brothers and sisters are in the house.*
7. *Your parents are in the living room, but your brother is in the kitchen because he is hungry.*
8. *We want to go to the dining room because we want to have dinner now.*
9. *I am in my bed because I am not able to (I cannot) work today.*
10. *The cat is on the table.*

LESSON 137

1. **trabajando** *(working)*
2. **hablando** *(speaking)*
3. **desayunando** *(having breakfast)*
4. **comiendo** *(eating)*
5. **bebiendo** *(drinking)*
6. **viendo** *(seeing)*
7. **caminando** *(walking)*
8. **teniendo** *(having)*

LESSON 138

1. *I am buying.*
2. *You are eating.*
3. *He is eating in the living room.*
4. *She is buying a car.*
5. *We are not eating.*
6. *Are y'all eating in the living room?*
7. *They are eating in the kitchen.*
8. *They are buying clothes.*
9. *We are able to (we can) eat in the dining room.*
10. *The dog is in the bedroom on the bed.*

LESSON 139

1. *I am cooking in the kitchen.*
2. *You are cooking the food.*
3. *My brother wants to cook dinner every night.*
4. *I cook every night, but tonight I want to go to a restaurant to have dinner.*
5. *They are hungry because they never have breakfast.*
6. *Your food is not on the table; it is on the desk.*
7. *We are in the living room.*
8. *She cooks every night.*
9. *He is not able to (he cannot) cook today; we need to have lunch at a restaurant.*
10. *My bed is in my bedroom.*

LESSON 140

1. *I am making dinner.*
2. *She makes lunch every day.*
3. *He goes to the library every day to do his work.*
4. *We are making breakfast right now.*
5. *I have breakfast every morning, but you never have breakfast.*
6. *They always make dinner.*
7. *Do you make breakfast every morning?*
8. *I always do my work OR I always do my job.*
9. *He is cooking the food in the kitchen, but I am in my bedroom.*
10. *I am having dinner in my bedroom tonight.*

LESSON 141

1. *I want to make lunch for my friends.*
2. *My father does not want to buy a car for my brother.*
3. *My parents go to the store to buy food every week.*
4. *We are buying a dog for the children.*
5. *I make food for my friends every week.*
6. *You make food for your dogs every day.*
7. *My brother is making dinner for his children.*
8. *My mother is cooking the food right now.*
9. *The children are in the bed now.*
10. *I always carry books and I go to the library to read every day.*

LESSON 142

1. *I sleep in my bed every night.*
2. *She is sleeping in her bed with her cats.*
3. *The cat sleeps in the living room every night.*
4. *I do not want to go to the beach; I want to sleep in my bed.*
5. *The children are sleeping.*
6. *She is cooking food for her family.*
7. *We are not able to (we cannot) go to the park because we are having lunch right now.*
8. *Do you have a desk in your bedroom?*
9. *No, but I have a table in my living room.*
10. *My mother is making dinner right now; she makes dinner every night.*

LESSON 143

1. *There is a dog in the house.*
2. *There are two desks in my bedroom.*
3. *There are some children at the park.*
4. *There is a cat on the table.*
5. *There is food in the kitchen.*
6. *The children are sleeping in the bed.*
7. *I need to eat right now!*
8. *I always do my work OR I always do my job.*
9. *Every night my cat goes to my bedroom to sleep in the bed with me.*
10. *My children want to cook dinner tonight.*

LESSON 147

1. *I don't like my food.*
2. *I don't like my mother's cats.*
3. *You don't like the food.*
4. *You don't like cats.*
5. *He likes the beach* OR *She likes the beach* OR *It likes the beach.* (In the context of formal speech, this could also mean *You like the beach.*)
6. *I am not able to (I cannot) sleep because I do not like the bed.*
7. *We like the restaurant, but we are not hungry.*
8. *There are some young men at the beach.*
9. *They like the book* OR *Y'all like the book* (depending on the context).
10. *I am doing my work, but you are always sleeping.*

LESSON 148

1. *The young woman likes the food.*
2. *Your father likes books.*
3. *The men like the food.*
4. *I do not like the park.*
5. *Dad likes his friend's car.*
6. *The young women like the mall.*
7. *Your family likes the beach.*
8. *I make dinner every night, but you are always sleeping in your bedroom.*
9. *I like to cook.*
10. *There are some books on your desk.*

LESSON 149

1. *I like the food.*
2. *You like dogs.*
3. *You like the beach.*
4. *She likes the restaurant.*
5. *We like cats.*
6. *Y'all don't like my car.*
7. *They like the mall.*
8. *My father is making his lunch.*
9. *There is a cat in my bedroom and it is sleeping on my bed.*
10. *My father does his work every day* OR *My father does his job every day.*

LESSON 150

1. *Does she like my car?*
2. *Does she like my car?*
3. *Do they like to have breakfast every morning?*
4. *Do they like to have lunch every day?*
5. *Do you like my books?*
6. *Do you like to go to the mall?*
7. *Do they like to cook?*
8. *We like to go to the beach.*
9. *I am cooking dinner in the kitchen.*
10. *We often carry money.*

LESSON 151

1. *I love the beach.*
2. *My father loves my house.*
3. *I love to have dinner with my family.*
4. *You love to have dinner at a restaurant every night.*
5. *She loves to buy clothes at the mall.*
6. *They love to go to the beach often* OR *Y'all love to go to the beach often* (depending on the context)
7. *Do they like to cook?*
8. *You don't like to eat at restaurants.*
9. *Is there food in your kitchen?*
10. *Are you able to (can you) work today?*

LESSON 152

1. *I love to eat eggs.*
2. *My mom likes to cook eggs.*
3. *Y'all love to have eggs for breakfast.*
4. *Are the eggs in the kitchen?*
5. *We need to buy some eggs tomorrow.*
6. *They love eggs.*
7. *He loves my mother's food.*
8. *We are not able to (we cannot) go to the mall because we are having lunch now.*
9. *There is an egg on the table.*
10. *You are not able to (you cannot) sleep because you do not like the bed.*

LESSON 153

1. *I want eggs, please.*
2. *We want to eat now, please.*
3. *Are you able to (can you) make breakfast for me, please?*
4. *I like to be at the library.*
5. *They like to go to the beach every week.*
6. *Do y'all like to eat eggs?*
7. *They like to read my father's books often.*
8. *I need to make breakfast for my children now.*
9. *I love the park. Do you like the park also?*
10. *The dog wants my dinner.*

LESSON 154

1. *More water, please.*
2. *There is more food in the kitchen.*
3. *I want more eggs, please.*
4. *Please, are you able to (can you) cook more eggs?*
5. *We love your mother's food.*
6. *Y'all need to read more books.*
7. *My brother needs to drink more water.*
8. *The cat is in the kitchen and he is sleeping on the table.*
9. *I also want to have lunch.*
10. *My mother is making dinner for my father.*

LESSON 155

1. *Thank you.*
2. *You're welcome.*
3. *Thank you for the food, Mom.*
4. *You're welcome, my son.*
5. *Thank you for the clothes, Dad.*
6. *You're welcome, my daughter.*
7. *We need more food, please.*
8. *My sisters do not like eggs.*
9. *Do you like eggs?*
10. *No, I do not like eggs.*

LESSON 156

1. *Thank you for making breakfast, Mom.*
2. *Thank you for walking to the beach with me.*
3. *Thank you for making food for my friends.*
4. *Thank you for going to the store and buying the food.*
5. *Please, I need more water.*
6. *My dog loves to sleep on my bed.*
7. *We love to eat in restaurants.*
8. *We want to sleep right now.*
9. *You are not able to (you cannot) sleep because your dogs and your cats sleep in the bed with you every night.*
10. *He loves his desk.*

LESSON 157

1. *Thank you for the cereal.*
2. *We want cereal with milk.*
3. *I want to have cereal with milk for breakfast, please.*
4. *I love milk with my cereal.*
5. *There is cereal in the kitchen.*
6. *Do y'all want to drink milk?*
7. *Thank you for making my lunch, Dad.*
8. *My brother does not like eggs, but he likes cereal with milk.*
9. *Are you eating breakfast right now?*
10. *I am not able to (I cannot) carry the books to school every morning.*

LESSON 158

1. *Do you want toast with butter?*
2. *I like my toast without butter.*
3. *I want more toast, please.*
4. *Thank you for making my toast, Mom.*
5. *I do not want cereal; I want toast with butter, please.*
6. *Do y'all want more milk?*
7. *I love to have toast with butter for breakfast every morning.*
8. *They like to eat eggs and toast every morning.*
9. *Thank you for working every day, Dad.*
10. *Y'all are not able to (y'all cannot) buy clothes at the mall without money.*

LESSON 159

1. *She wants coffee, but I want juice.*
2. *More juice, please.*
3. *Thank you for making the coffee.*
4. *My father is making coffee for my mother.*
5. *I am not able to (I cannot) sleep because I am drinking coffee.*
6. *I love to drink coffee with my breakfast.*
7. *We drink coffee every morning.*
8. *We want to have eggs, cereal, milk and toast with butter for breakfast.*
9. *My dad makes breakfast every morning; he is making breakfast right now.*
10. *Do you like your coffee with milk?*

LESSON 160

1. *We need to eat more fruit every day.*
2. *My brother does not like to eat oranges.*
3. *Do y'all want more fruit?*
4. *The oranges are in the kitchen on the table.*
5. *My children love to eat oranges.*
6. *We do not need to sleep right now; we need to drink coffee because we need to work.*
7. *Thank you for the cereal and the toast.*
8. *My son likes toast with butter.*
9. *I am not able to (I cannot) drink milk, but I love juice.*
10. *My friends are walking to the park.*

LESSON 162

1. *I love to eat salads.*
2. *I want to have soup and salad for lunch.*
3. *Thank you for making a salad.*
4. *My cat is on the table and he is hungry.*
5. *I want to drink orange juice with my breakfast.*
6. *My children love toast with butter.*
7. *More coffee, please.*
8. *She is not able to (she cannot) go to the park because she is having lunch with her family right now.*
9. *My children have breakfast every morning with me.*
10. *Mr. Smith wants to have soup for lunch every day, but Mrs. Smith likes to have fruit and salad for lunch.*

LESSON 163

1. *Do you want to have chicken for lunch?*
2. *Yes, I want chicken soup.*
3. *My mother always cooks chicken soup.*
4. *The turkey is in the kitchen on the table.*
5. *My mom and my dad are cooking a turkey.*
6. *We never eat cereal without milk.*
7. *My parents like to have toast and coffee for breakfast every morning.*
8. *I am not able to (I cannot) drink milk, but I am able to (I can) drink orange juice.*
9. *We always carry fruit.*
10. *The young women want to go to the library today because they need more books.*

LESSON 164

1. *I have a sandwich for lunch every day.*
2. *He wants a turkey sandwich.*
3. *Do you want a chicken sandwich?*
4. *My friend is eating a sandwich, but I am drinking coffee.*
5. *My family loves to have eggs, fruit, and cereal with milk for breakfast.*
6. *We have lunch every day, but we never eat sandwiches.*
7. *I am thirsty and I want to drink orange juice.*
8. *My mother does not like milk in her coffee.*
9. *There is a chicken sandwich in the dining room.*
10. *Do you like your toast with butter?*

LESSON 165

1. *My mother is cooking chicken, vegetables and potatoes for dinner.*
2. *My dad loves potatoes.*
3. *Mom, I do not want to eat vegetables.*
4. *My children do not like vegetables.*
5. *I like turkey sandwiches.*
6. *The restaurant has soups, salads and sandwiches.*
7. *Today we are having fruit for breakfast.*
8. *My dad wants to have a chicken sandwich for lunch, but I want chicken soup.*
9. *Do you like orange juice?*
10. *No, I do not like orange juice, but I love to drink coffee.*

LESSON 166

1. *More rice and more salad, please.*
2. *We always have chicken and rice for dinner, but we have turkey sandwiches for lunch.*
3. *We do not have rice but we have bread.*
4. *We drink orange juice every morning.*
5. *You are able to (you can) make a turkey sandwich because we have bread and turkey.*
6. *I like oranges but I do not like vegetables.*
7. *We are not able to (we cannot) make chicken soup because we do not have chicken.*
8. *My mother is making a fruit salad, but I do not like salads.*
9. *You are not able to (you cannot) go to school without your books.*
10. *The cat sees my soup, and he is hungry.*

LESSON 168

1. *The book is new.*
2. *My parents have a new house.*
3. *I love Mr. Smith's new restaurant.*
4. *I like to read new books.*
5. *The soup is in the kitchen.*
6. *We need a new dog.*
7. *Jennifer, Megan and Ashley are my new friends.*
8. *My brother wants to have a turkey sandwich and soup for lunch.*
9. *We have chicken, rice and bread for dinner every night.*
10. *Y'all are not able to (y'all cannot) make a salad because y'all do not have vegetables.*

LESSON 169

1. *I am not hungry because my chicken sandwich is old.*
2. *The old women are my mother's friends.*
3. *The library does not have old books.*
4. *My father wants a new job.*
5. *My old dog is in the dining room.*
6. *My mom does not like to drink old coffee.*
7. *The library is old but the books are new.*
8. *The potatoes are old and also the vegetables.*
9. *My children love chicken soup.*
10. *The dog wants to sleep in my bed with me every night.*

LESSON 170

1. *My sandwich is very old.*
2. *Your father is very old.*
3. *My clothes are very old.*
4. *My daughters' school is new.*
5. *We have an old car but we need a new car.*
6. *My children do not like to read old books, but they love new books.*
7. *I want to go to a new restaurant tonight.*
8. *We eat bread often.*
9. *We cannot sleep because we do not like the new bed.*
10. *I am making dinner for my friends.*

LESSON 171

1. *This car is very new.*
2. *These eggs are very old.*
3. *This salad is old.*
4. *These potatoes are very old.*
5. *I want to buy this new car.*
6. *My children do not like these vegetables.*
7. *My friend wants to eat a sandwich.*
8. *Sir, I do not like this salad.*
9. *We love turkey sandwiches.*
10. *Do you drink orange juice every day?*

LESSON 172

1. *That car is a new car.*
2. *Those men are my friends.*
3. *That soup is very old.*
4. *Those young women are my sisters.*
5. *Do you want to buy that car?*
6. *Thank you for making this sandwich.*
7. *There is an old potato on the table.*
8. *My father wants to buy this car.*
9. *My children do not like to sleep in that bed.*
10. *That woman has five children.*

LESSON 173

1. *Your car is beautiful.*
2. *My mother is very beautiful.*
3. *Those dogs are beautiful.*
4. *Mrs. Smith is beautiful.*
5. *These young women are very beautiful.*
6. *These clothes are my sister's new clothes.*
7. *He needs to buy a new car.*
8. *My children are not able to (cannot) drink orange juice.*
9. *This cat is drinking milk.*
10. *My brother is in that house.*

LESSON 174

1. *This soup is cold.*
2. *Those potatoes are very hot.*
3. *Thank you for the cold water.*
4. *This food is hot.*
5. *My children like cold milk.*
6. *She wants to go to the mall because she wants to buy new clothes.*
7. *The old man does not like to cook.*
8. *We have these three beautiful daughters.*
9. *The restaurant has cold sandwiches.*
10. *My egg is cold.*

LESSON 175

1. *You have that big house, but we have this small house.*
2. *He has a large and beautiful house.*
3. *My dog has a small bed, but he wants to sleep in my bed with me every night.*
4. *My cat is very small and he likes to drink hot milk.*
5. *My sister does not want this small car; she wants that big car.*
6. *I do not like these old cars.*
7. *Mr. Jones is buying a new house today.*
8. *Those eggs are very hot.*
9. *I eat fruit every morning.*
10. *I see a beautiful woman at the bank every week.*

LESSON 176

1. *My brother does not like cheap clothes.*
2. *My clothes are very expensive.*
3. *That restaurant has cheap food, but the food is old.*
4. *My father has an expensive car.*
5. *They always carry those big books to school.*
6. *I am not able to (I cannot) eat this food because it is very cold.*
7. *I want a small salad with my dinner.*
8. *Is the soup hot?*
9. *My mother is old and she has a very old car.*
10. *Is this new car expensive?*

LESSON 177

1. *Mr. Jones has a lot of money.*
2. *We have many books.*
3. *Today we are doing a lot of work.*
4. *There are many sandwiches in the kitchen.*
5. *My dog drinks a lot of water every day.*
6. *There are many children at the school.*
7. *The library has many expensive books.*
8. *My mother is making a lot of bread.*
9. *Thank you for buying this cheap book.*
10. *Goodbye, friends.*

PRONUNCIATION GUIDE

This abbreviated guide to Spanish pronunciation will provide a few of the most important points to keep in mind when pronouncing Spanish words.

VOWELS

a sounds like the **a** in *father*
e sounds like the **e** in *bet*
i sounds like the **ee** in *meet*
o sounds like the **o** in *obey*
u usually sounds like the **u** in *rule*

CONSONANTS

g sounds like the **g** in *go*, except when it comes before **i** or **e**. Then, **g** sounds similar to the **h** in *happy* (but with a more "breathy" sound)
h is always silent
j sounds similar to the **h** in *happy* (but with a more "breathy" sound)
ñ sounds like the **ny** in *canyon*
r should be slightly and quickly rolled, sounding like the **d** in *ladder*
rr should be heavily rolled
s is always a hissing **s** sound as in the word *mess*, never a **z** sound as in *is*
z is always a hissing **s** sound as in the word *mess*, never a **z** sound as in *is*

GLOSSARY

a *to* (lesson 87, 89)

a menudo *often* (lesson 92)

adiós *goodbye* (lesson 25)

agua *water* (lesson 72)

ahora *now* (lesson 128)

ahora mismo *right now* (lesson 128)

almorzar *to have lunch* (lesson 127)

almuerzo *I have lunch* (lesson 127)

amiga *friend* (female) (lesson 15)

amigo *friend* (male) (lesson 15)

arroz *rice* (lesson 166)

barato *cheap* (lesson 176)

beber *to drink* (lesson 81)

bebo *I drink* (lesson 81)

biblioteca *library* (lesson 120)

buenas noches *good evening / good night* (lesson 25)

buenas tardes *good afternoon* (lesson 25)

buenos días *good morning* (lesson 25)

café *coffee* (lesson 159)

caliente *hot* (lesson 174)

cama *bed* (lesson 136)

caminar *to walk* (lesson 103)

camino *I walk* (lesson 103)

cargar *to carry* (lesson 116)

cargo *I carry* (lesson 116)

caro *expensive* (lesson 176)

carro *car* (lesson 62)

casa *house* (lesson 134)

cenar *to have dinner* (lesson 129)

ceno *I have dinner* (lesson 129)

centro comercial *mall* (lesson 91)

cereal *cereal* (lesson 157)

cero *zero* (lesson 42)

cocina *kitchen* (lesson 135)

cocino *I cook* (lesson 139)

cocinar *to cook* (lesson 139)

cinco *five* (lesson 42)

comedor *dining room* (lesson 135)

comer *to eat* (lesson 80)

comida *food* (lesson 70)

como *I eat* (lesson 80)

comprar *to buy* (lesson 105)

compro *I buy* (lesson 77)

con *with* (lesson 84)

conmigo *with me* (lesson 85)

contigo *with you* (lesson 85)

cuatro *four* (lesson 42)

de *of, from* (lesson 60, 61, 161)

de nada *you're welcome* (lesson 155)

desayunar *to have breakfast* (lesson 125)

desayuno (verb) *I have breakfast* (lesson 125)

desayuno (noun) *breakfast* (lesson 125)

día *day* (lesson 76)

diez *ten* (lesson 43)

dinero *money* (lesson 47)

doce *twelve* (lesson 43)

dólar *dollar* (lesson 48)

dormir *to sleep* (lesson 142)

dos *two* (lesson 42)

duermo *I sleep* (lesson 142)

el *the* (lesson 3)

él *he* (lesson 32)

ella *she* (lesson 32)

ellos / ellas *they* (lesson 37)

emparedado *sandwich* (lesson 164)

en *in, at, on* (lesson 132)

ensalada *salad* (lesson 162)

eres *you are* (lesson 31)

es *he is, she is, it is* (lesson 33)

escritorio *desk* (lesson 133)

escuela *school* (lesson 114)

ese *that* (lesson 172)

español Spanish (lesson 74)

este *this* (lesson 171)

estar *to be* (lesson 131)

estoy *I am* (lesson 131)

familia *family* (lesson 101)

frío *cold* (lesson 174)

fruta *fruit* (lesson 160)

gato *cat* (lesson 44)

gracias *thank you* (lesson 155)

grande *large* (lesson 175)

gustar *to be pleasing* (lesson 145)

habitación *bedroom* (lesson 136)

hablar *to speak* (lesson 74)

hablo *I speak* (lesson 74)
hacer *to do, to make* (lesson 140)
hago *I do, I make* (lesson 140)
hambre *hunger* (lesson 65)
hay *there is, there are* (lesson 143)
hermano *brother* (lesson 9)
hermana *sister* (lesson 11)
hermoso *beautiful* (lesson 173)
hija *daughter* (lesson 23)
hijo *son* (lesson 23)
hola *hello* (lesson 25)
hombre *man* (lesson 21)
hoy *today* (lesson 109)
huevo *egg* (lesson 152)
iglesia *church* (lesson 119)
inglés *English* (lesson 74)
ir *to go* (lesson 86)
jugo *juice* (lesson 159)
la *the* (lesson 5)
las *the* (lesson 20)
leche *milk* (lesson 157)
leer *to read* (lesson 117)
leo *I read* (lesson 117)
los *the* (lesson 20)
libro *book* (lesson 115)
madre *mother* (lesson 26)
mamá *mom* (lesson 26)
mañana *tomorrow* (lesson 111)
mantequilla *butter* (lesson 158)
más *more* (lesson 154)
me encanta *I love* (lesson 151)
me gusta *I like* (lesson 146)
mesa *table* (lesson 133)
mi *my* (lesson 12)
muchacha *young woman, girl* (lesson 16)
muchacho *young man, boy* (lesson 16)
mucho *much, many* (lesson 177)
muy *very* (lesson 170)
mujer *woman* (lesson 21)
naranja *orange* (lesson 160)
necesitar *to need* (lesson 110)
necesito *I need* (lesson 110)
niña *girl* (lesson 6)
niño *boy* (lesson 4)

no *not* (lesson 30), *no* (lesson 79)

nosotros/nosotras *we* (lesson 35)

nueve *nine* (lesson 43)

nuevo *new* (lesson 168)

nunca *never* (lesson 93)

ocho *eight* (lesson 43)

once *eleven* (lesson 43)

padre *father* (lesson 26)

pan *bread* (lesson 166)

papa *potato* (lesson 165)

papá *dad* (lesson 26)

para *for, for the purpose of, in order to* (lesson 122, 141)

parque *park* (lesson 95)

pavo *turkey* (lesson 163)

periódico *newspaper* (lesson 118)

pequeño *small* (lesson 175)

pero *but* (lesson 51)

perro *dog* (lesson 44)

playa *beach* (lesson 96)

poder *to be able* (lesson 112)

pollo *chicken* (lesson 163)

por *for* (lesson 156)

por favor *please* (lesson 153)

porque *because* (lesson 71)

puedo *I am able* (lesson 112)

querer *to want* (lesson 66)

quiero *I want* (lesson 66)

restaurante *restaurant* (lesson 123)

ropa *clothes* (lesson 108)

sala *living room* (lesson 135)

sed *thirst* (lesson 65)

seis *six* (lesson 42)

semana *week* (lesson 82)

señor *Mr., sir* (lesson 34)

señora *Mrs., ma'am* (lesson 34)

señorita *Miss* (lesson 34)

siempre *always* (lesson 75)

sí *yes* (lesson 79)

siete *seven* (lesson 43)

sin *without* (lesson 94)

sois *y'all are* (lesson 36)

somos *we are* (lesson 35)

son *they are* (lesson 38)

sopa *soup* (lesson 162)

soy *I am* (lesson 29)

su *his, her, its* (lesson 58) *your* (lesson 102)

también *also* (lesson 46)

tener *to have* (lesson 45)

tengo *I have* (lesson 45)

todas las noches *every night* (lesson 124)

todas las semanas *every week* (lesson 82)

todas las mañanas *every morning* (lesson 126)

todos los días *every day* (lesson 76)

tostada *toast* (lesson 158)

trabajar *to work* (lesson 83)

trabajo *I work* (lesson 83)

trabajo *work, job* (lesson 100)

tres *three* (lesson 42)

tu *your* (lesson 13)

tú *you* (lesson 13)

un *a, an, one* (lesson 8)

una *a, an, one* (lesson 10)

unas *some, a few* (lesson 24)

uno *one* (lesson 42)

unos *some, a few* (lesson 24)

usted *you* (lesson 98)

ustedes *y'all* (lesson (99)

vegetal *vegetable* (lesson 165)

viejo *old* (lesson 169)

vosotros/vosotras *y'all* (lesson 36)

veo *I see* (lesson 88)

ver *to see* (lesson 88)

voy *I go* (lesson 86)

y *and* (lesson 7)

yo *I* (lesson 29)

SUBJECT INDEX

A

adjectives, lesson 167
article, lesson 1

C

conjugations, lesson 73

F

formal speech, lesson 97

G

gender, lesson 2
gerund, lesson 137, 138

I

idiom, lesson 64
infinitive, lesson 104
informal speech, lesson 97

N

number, lesson 17

P

person, lesson 40
personal endings, lesson 56
plural, lesson 17
possession, lesson 59
pronoun, lesson 28, 63
purpose, lesson 121, 122

Q

questions, lesson 78

S

singular, lesson 17
subject, lesson 27

T

titles, lesson 34

V

verb, lesson 27
verb stem, lesson 56, 67, 107

CPSIA information can be obtained at www.ICGtesting.com
Printed in the USA
LVOW13s0815170813

348306LV00001B/10/P